PRAISE FOR BETTER THAN PERFECT

Kristen's ability to present in a simple way the challenges of perfectionism and how it is possible to start to live a life we would love is a synthesis of a lifelong devoted to those she has chosen to help. Being a Pain Physiotherapist, I welcome this book as an aid to explore and discover ways to overcome the challenge of perfectionism.

—Shelley Barlow
PhD, Pain Physiotherapist and Psychotherapist,
Masters Gestalt Therapy (Brisbane)

A gifted coach with a generous heart, Kristen offers guidance, mentoring, and an empathic ear to those who seek to throw off their shackles and shine. The pragmatic wisdom delivered in *Better than Perfect* offers a simple yet profound path for seekers of wholehearted living.

—Judy Brightman
Instructor, Master and
nal Reiki practitioner,
Mindfulness/Personal/
Dach, Somatic Coach.
rsemindfulleader.com

This book
read for everyone.

—Shelley Rosenburg
Founding member of Eponaquest Equine Facilitated
Experiential Learning (EFL)
and the International Equine Summit,
Author of *My Horses My Healers, Accessing Your Intuition*

Kristen shows us in her book how to reduce the volume of the inner critic's voice to be able to connect to our intuition and follow our heart to find our purpose. Her techniques are simple yet highly effective.

—Penny Leonard
North Coast Writer

BETTER THAN PERFECT

FREE YOUR MIND,
FIND YOUR PURPOSE,
FOLLOW YOUR PASSION

KRISTEN ABLESON

Published by Author Academy Elite
PO Box 43, Powell, OH 43065
www.AuthorAcademyElite.com

Identifiers:
ISBN: 979-8-88583-026-3 (paperback)
ISBN: 979-8-88583-027-0 (hardback)
ISBN: 979-8-88583-028-7 (ebook)

Available in paperback, hardback, e-book, and audiobook

CONTENTS

FOR THE READER

"There has to be more to life!"

If you've uttered those words in a desperate wish to gain a wider view of the world—one that allows you to see past the narrow lens of perfectionism—this book is for you. I believe you can shift your view from a life that focused on being perfect and in control (and consequently filled with constant anger and criticism) to one that recognizes the limitation of perfectionism and see another, *better* way to live.

If you are tired of the way life always seems to turn out—sick of the same types of relationships, the same reactions to others, and the seeming inability to stay on focus and follow your dreams—you have picked up the right book. *Better than Perfect* explores practices in which the perfectionists' beliefs have set up addictive patterns that, with our thoughts, Inner Critic, feelings, and body reactions, create those limiting ways in which we are in the world. This book focuses on processes where we can move forward and past all of it.

The setup in chapters throughout *Better than Perfect* moves through major facets of the perfectionists' beliefs and behaviors to show you the power of the perfectionist mindset and how limiting and controlling it can be. It shows you the way we see others with respect to this lens and the mask that we strive to maintain and discloses just how these affect our relationships with others, our lives, and even ourselves.

Sometimes it seems impossible to see life in any other way, but there *is* another way. In this book, I will not only reveal these forms of addictions but will also show you how to break them down and change them so they no longer have power and no longer take us off the path. There is a path that we want to be on which is difficult to see and hear let alone follow if our perfectionist ways are so loud and powerful.

The various techniques described in this book offer a way to finally free yourself from the addictive power of perfectionism. I've even included homework* to help you practice the techniques that reduce these addictive patterns. As you apply what you learn, you will break the habits that limit your life. You'll discover how to hear your inner intuition that is a lot quieter in nature than your perfectionist beliefs and perceptions. When you can hear it, you can start to follow it and live more in a place of flow being in the life you have dreamt of, a life involving your heart and higher purpose instead of in a life of control, anger, and trying to be perfect. You can finally live a life of growth and learn to reach your full potential rather than stay scared of failure and critical of the things that don't really matter. Finally, you can be fully in the world instead of being overwhelmed and anxious by it.

It's time to free your mind, find your purpose, and follow your passion.

Start reading and take the first step toward becoming the person you were meant to be.

---

* If you've suffered trauma in the past or if the homework exercises seem overwhelming, then it may be helpful to practice them with a supportive professional.

To Gain the Most from This Book

You will find a Homework section at the end of each chapter. I suggest that you complete the homework before moving on to the next chapter to best assimilate what you've learned.

I have also created two guided visualizations, one on *groundedness* and one to help you refocus and dream, in addition to the companion workbook which you can use in conjunction with the homework. To access these *free* downloadable resources, please use the following link:

https://linktr.ee/kristenableson

1

FEEL THE PAIN AND DO IT ANYWAY

Don't let the fear of failure stop you; the world needs your greatness.

—Emmanuel Apetsi

Whatever it is I need to do, I feel like I have to do it perfectly. It's hard to deal with the constant need to be correct and desire to do the perfect thing all the time. It's my desire to be the perfect person in every situation—knowledgeable of everything all the time, complete, smiling, open, caring, not angry, not emotional, a great listener, and whatever else it takes to just be perfect all of the time. My Inner Critic maintains constant vigilance and requires me to control my emotions and always keep them in check.

As I work for perfection, nothing pains me more than to see others who don't know that *perfection* is and should always be the goal. I mean, aren't they aware that everyone should strive to be the best, be more, and be perfect? Do they not know that life is about being correct, following the rules, and making sure that those things are all done or addressed before considering anything non-essential (i.e., any sort of enjoyment). Until everything essential is completed, all pleasure should be denied. Life consists of monitoring ourselves, avoiding making mistakes that others can see, controlling ourselves, and keeping it all together.

These are some of the unconscious mottos of the perfectionist. Although we each have our unique way as individuals to see and be in this world, a core driver for perfectionism is to seek perfection. When describing the personality of the perfectionist in her book *The Enneagram*, Helen Palmer writes:

> "Perfectionists are usually not aware that they deny themselves pleasure. They are so preoccupied with what they "should" do and "what must be done" that they rarely ask themselves what they want to get out of life. They learn to block out desires by focusing attention on the correct thing to do."[1]

Is seeking perfection all there is? There has to be more to life than this. How heavy and all-consuming is this negativity! Surely life is meant to be lighter and more fun? I want more fun; I want more laughs and amazement. There must be another way.

So, what's the answer? Is there another way to follow our dreams and succeed in the flow instead of following the rules and judging others and ourselves for not being perfect? How can we follow the pleasures in life, find joy in "wasting time," and connect to our heart's desires? Can we actually get what we want? This has to be possible, right?

I've learned from my experience as a physiotherapist, as a facilitator of an equestrian program, Leadership with Horses, which shines a light on people's blocks as well as the inner qualities they can tap into strengthen and empower their own leadership abilities, and from observing and working on myself that people have their own set of perceptions, beliefs, thoughts, and feelings about the world they encounter. The way people experience the world is what they base their decisions on and contributes to their behaviors. There are common beliefs that people can embrace in varying degrees, like being worthy, being good enough, having capacity, and belonging. There are many more. Everyone has a unique combination of these beliefs and thus their own individual view of the world that allows them to function in it. Perfectionists have a combination of beliefs; our perfection belief is at our core. With this belief comes certain qualities of being a perfectionist. These then become the drivers of our behaviors and habits. All of these are unconscious until we become aware of them and how they govern and direct our behaviors, actions, and lives.

They are repetitive and consistent. And they are very limiting.

All humans are driven by a combination of beliefs and a higher part, guided by their intuition. Working with this premise, people refer to their higher part using a variety of terms, including higher perspective, higher purpose, higher self, heart's desire, soul, greater intelligence, higher being, bigger self, authentic self, or simply as dreams. Our intuition is the voice of our higher part, the first thought we hear before our rational minds take over—before we question it with our logic and belief system. Our intuition is often quickly overrun by our belief system and loud Inner Critics' voice, so it can be difficult to hear if we don't know it's there and how to listen to it.

Whichever has the loudest voice or is the strongest in intensity is the one we hear and notice. This determines what path we take and what we think is important.

Figure A

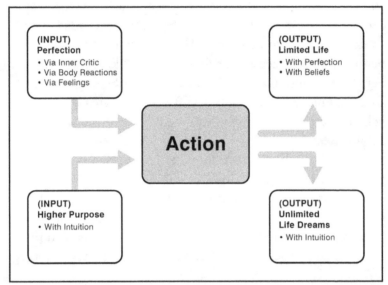

Figure A is a summary of the inputs and outputs that determine our behavior. The action we take depends on which input we follow. If we listen to and act on the input from our Inner Critic, thoughts, body reactions, and feelings, these perfectionist beliefs limit our lives. If we listen to and take action on our intuition, we move toward a life guided by our higher purpose. Our actions determine our paths in life, and our inputs determine our actions.

WHAT DOES PERFECTIONISM LOOK LIKE?

Perfectionists feel we have to be perfect in every situation, with everybody, and with everything we do. Life is about monitoring ourselves and avoiding making mistakes others can see.

We like structure; we want things to be balanced, like the wall hangings that need to be straight and the walking cadence that needs to be even.

The list goes on.

- We are quite righteous.
- There is a right way to do things, and we know it.

- We like rules.

- We hate conflict.

- We churn constantly.

- Things need to be said perfectly with the correct words and intonation.

- We judge.

- We control.

- We are angry a lot of the time, yet it's not perfect to show emotion, so it is perfectly hidden—hence, we can use a large amount of passive aggression and sarcasm.

- We believe you can't see through our perfect mask.

- We find it hard to start a task.

- Procrastination is our best friend.

- It's also hard to complete a task because it's never perfect.

- We have a harsh Inner Critic—our inner voice likes to tell us everything we cannot do. It just loves to compare us to perfection, judging our lack by comparison. It feels as invasive as an external source even though it is actually us.

On the other hand, my higher purpose—or higher part of me—just wants me to be the person I was born to be, follow my heart, be in the flow, live my life to the fullest, and connect with others from this space.

To help explain this further, consider the following example. If my higher purpose was to empower people to be the leaders of their own lives and help them follow their dreams, then I need to be able to communicate my message effectively to them. I need to get my message and information out into the world. There are many avenues to achieve this, and speaking on stage would be one of them; there are many ways, but I am using this way to illustrate my point.

Helping people follow their dreams is my higher purpose. To speak on stage with effectiveness, I would have to battle my Inner Critic's view of what that looks like and my perfectionist rules. The limiting part of me would prefer I didn't speak on stage. It wants me to stay small and not expose myself to potential failure. How am I supposed to be my authentic self, living in my higher purpose, teaching and sharing wisdom with others by speaking on stage if my Inner Critic and perfectionist qualities feel it's a bad idea?

Perfectionism viewpoint (unconscious and powerfully limiting)

- If I do this, I will fail.

- The criticism from myself and others will be too much to bear—I could die.

- Others will finally have proof that I'm not perfect, thus proving my deepest fear that I have spent all my life trying to cover up. I am not perfect.

By following our perfectionistic ways, everything needs to be done correctly. Our entire focus from this viewpoint is not to fail, and from this, people will never know we're not perfect. If I manage to deliver the speech, the Inner Critic will commentate on everything and find something to focus on that means it wasn't perfect. Often, this focus can be irrelevant to the outcome of what I was trying to achieve—like every person didn't laugh at the appropriate time or one word was out of place—but I still failed. As I said, the Inner Critic is harsh. Anything could be viewed as failing. It will attack everything, and the details it focuses on may have absolutely no bearing on the success of the speech. One insignificant detail—like a man in the audience looking at his watch—can be made the focus of the entire speech. He looked at his watch, and thus, I perceived he wasn't interested. This can then earn an incredibly overpowering failure mark. Failure is bad. Failure is to be avoided.

From this viewpoint, keeping me from potential failure is imperative to keeping me and my secret safe, and keeping me small, so no one finds out my secret—that I'm not perfect. My viewpoint is, therefore, limiting and controlling.

We may also show imperfection and leak emotions as we may not be able to control them, like over-the-top excitement, anger, or sarcasm—anything that can be criticized. For our own safety, it's best to stay small and not do it. As this is a safety thing, my perfectionism viewpoint will do its utmost to avoid anything that can be interpreted as not perfect. It will do everything in its power to stop me from being in my heart, being open and exposed, and following my higher purpose. It wants to stop me from getting on that stage.

In my life, perfectionism has stopped me from Stepping Up in its own unique way, from giving me such anxiety that I can't find the words to speak properly to body pains giving me headaches and watery eyes. The loud Inner Critic has even disabled my ability to remember what I'm trying to say, longing to be finished. I miss the joy of expression as I cut my story short just to get off stage as soon as possible. From never having the perfect outcome, never delivering the speech perfectly, not getting the appropriate reaction from everyone, or whatever it has decided is the perfect outcome, it misinterprets my growth and ongoing attempts and learnings as consistent failure. There's no room to improve because my thoughts aren't encouraged to try, and therefore, there's no opportunity to practice and grow during the speech.

On the other hand, my higher self doesn't care about pass or fail, and it certainly doesn't care what others think—it just wants me to be my authentic self, to grow and follow my dreams. As failing is necessary for growth, it stands to reason that to be the person I am meant to be would mean trying, failing, learning, and growing. This is essential to follow my heart's desire and reach my dream. Failing here isn't a bad thing—it's actually essential to be more effective and to be all that I want to be. Failing here is a tool, and it is desired.

My focus shifts away from the insignificant detail that someone looked at their watch—that doesn't lead to me learning, growing, and being more effective at delivering my message—to the factors that enable me to achieve my higher purpose. That is, to be my authentic self, express valuable, helpful information to others, connect via being a compelling speaker, and ultimately empower people to be the leaders of their own lives. I'm looking for feedback and learnings to see if I achieved empowering people with enough knowledge and tools to succeed, as well as things I can improve on for next time. The focus isn't that I failed because everyone didn't laugh when I thought they should.

How do we make this delivery of information to follow my intuition and higher purpose easier and with more joy, fun, and effectiveness?

1) PRACTICE.

Stepping Up and following our intuition and higher purpose takes time and work. It's like a muscle that needs strengthening—it needs constant work to follow that dream. When the term *Stepping Up* is referenced in this book, it means to take action to follow your higher purpose when your limiting beliefs suggest otherwise.

When we move into the zone where the Inner Critic and our belief system feel we are unsafe, they will arc up to try and stop us. If we continue to show up and try, learn from our last effort, and put into action what we have learned, we gradually start to prove to ourselves that maybe the story about failure being bad and threatening to our being may not be entirely true. We start to gain awareness; we begin to question these notions that we've told ourselves for years—the focus of failing turns into a positive approach.

2) LEARN TO CALM THE MIND AND TURN DOWN THE VOLUME OF OUR INNER CRITIC.

Imagine if our Inner Critic was quiet, and all we could hear was our intuition. What a different world it would be! Unfortunately, this is generally not the case. The Inner Critic is very loud. If we listen only to our Inner Critic, then we miss out on opportunities to be in our higher, authentic selves and to be the people we were meant to be.

It does not make sense to our perfectionism and other beliefs that our higher purpose is urging us to fail. Our higher purpose keeps saying, "Come on! Give it a go and learn." Knowing the difference between the two messengers takes awareness and practice. We may confuse the two sometimes as the Inner Critic is clever and works out new ways to give us information, to keep us small, and to stop us. But that's ok. That's a given. Failure here is not important and learning is. We need to refocus, have some compassion, keep listening for our intuition, and keep moving forward. It's about learning to increase the volume of our intuition and decrease the noise of our Inner Critic. Then we need to trust our intuition and act on it. Chapters 2 and 3 will tell you how.

One aim of this book is to share various techniques that will help you dim the volume of the Inner Critic and mind, allowing you to hear your intuition better, refocus, and follow its direction.

As a note, *refocus* is a phrase used in this book to mean changing focus away from what we are listening to and our perfectionism traits to listening more to instructions from our intuition and our higher purpose so we can focus and move towards that.

3) BREAK DOWN PATTERNS AND REACTIONS FROM OUR BODIES.

Stepping Up doesn't always go easily as the Inner Critic is always there judging, but also, the body is giving you signs that it wants you to stop. Our thoughts from our Inner Critic create body reactions. Feelings can also create body reactions.

Feelings can include (but are not isolated to):

- Fear
- Anger
- Scared
- Terrified
- Shame
- Nervousness

In the above example, when stepping out on stage, my body reacts by tightening and giving me a headache. It makes my eyes water. I feel terrified that I will fail, and I am scared to look into the crowd. In fact, each time I stand on stage, the same thoughts and feelings occur, creating the same patterns of reactions in my body. These patterns of reactions in my body have been laid down since I was young and became progressively more ingrained with time. The three inputs—thoughts, feelings, and body reactions—cause discomfort, and unconsciously, we try to avoid this discomfort. I try to avoid time on stage as this will unconsciously prevent more pain, discomfort, and perceived lack of perfectionism.

When we Step Up against what our perfections model and what our Inner Critic think, and thus outside of our comfort zone, it starts to judge, telling us the same reasons why what we're trying to do is a bad idea. Our feelings are invoked, and our bodies react to the same thoughts and feelings in the same way. This becomes our behavior.

Body signs or body reactions include (but aren't isolated to):

- Body tightness
- Headaches
- Anxiety
- Shallow breathing
- Unable to hear because the voice of the Inner Critic is so loud
- Eyes watering
- Anger or loss of emotional control
- Shaky voice
- Control

Figure B

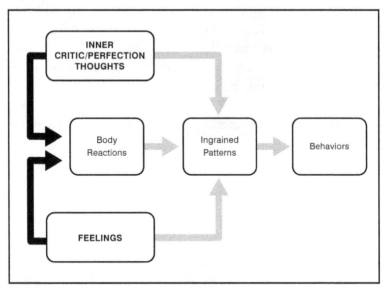

Figure B represents the three inputs that cause ingrained patterns creating our behaviors.

1. Thoughts cause reactions in the body (Body Reactions).

2. Feelings cause reactions in the body (Body Reactions).

3. The same thoughts and feelings ingrain and intensify these body reactions—the pathway becomes more ingrained.

With the same thoughts, feelings, and body reactions laid down over time, patterns in the body and our unique behaviors are formed.

These body reactions are ingrained and hard to deviate from. They can be bold and big and can make Stepping Up—or becoming our authentic higher selves—more difficult. Because the body reactions are uncomfortable, our priority becomes making this unpleasant thing go away. For example, I may limit my expression or time on stage. Our inputs can be loud or intense in reaction and help dim the volume of our intuition. Imagine what you could accomplish without having a headache on stage or your body getting tight every time you stepped up as your authentic self.

The aim is to break up these reaction patterns, to be less reactive and less triggered, thus making it easier to follow our intuition.

In Chapters 3, 4, 5, and 10, I discuss ways to help break up those patterns.

This process is the same for all people. The difference for perfectionists is that they have a common input—needing to be perfect. Though people have a unique set of behaviors due to their individual lived experiences, perfectionists' base behaviors can be similar (i.e., self-critical behavior, righteousness, and others listed on pages 7 and 8).

4) GROUNDEDNESS IS A WAY TO STEP OUT OF OUR THOUGHTS, FEELINGS, AND BODY REACTIONS AND HEAR OUR INTUITION.

John Prendergast explains in his book *In Touch* that "reality is inherently grounding. The more in touch with it we are, the more grounded we feel."

Being grounded is a way we can move outside of our patterns, thoughts, feelings, and body reactions. It enables us to take a step away from listening to our Inner Critic and perfectionist beliefs and into a space where it is easier to hear our intuition so it can guide us towards our dreams. Prendergast explains the metaphor of being *grounded*:

> The ground is both a metaphor and a felt sense. As a metaphor, it means to be in touch with reality. As a felt sense, it refers to feeling our center of gravity low in the belly and experiencing a deep silence, stability, and connection with the whole of life. Feeling grounded does not require contact with the earth; it can happen anywhere and anytime. Attention drops down from the head and into the trunk and core of the body. We can feel more of what is happening in the heart area and the gut.[2]

Figure C

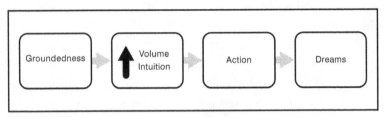

Figure C—The ability to ground yourself can place you outside of your thoughts, feelings, and body reactions, enabling you to hear your intuition as it is louder. There are many ways to feel grounded, sink into our bodies, and listen. These will be reviewed in greater detail as you progress through the book.

Here's one way to ground yourself using your imagination:

1) Close your eyes (only if it's safe to do so—otherwise, keep your eyes open).

2) Imagine roots are growing out of your feet. They grow deep into the ground.

3) Imagine them growing bigger and more solid.

4) Feel the solidness in your body.

5) Become aware of your breathing as you slow it down.

6) Keep breathing and imagining your legs growing thicker and heavier.

7) Feel the weight as you sink deeper into your legs.

8) Stay in this space for a few more breaths.

Notice how easy this technique is to do simply by engaging your imagination. It doesn't take long with this technique to feel and be more grounded and away from your Inner Critic, your body's reactions, and perfectionist beliefs and patterns. You'll begin to realize and feel when your body is tight and you're reacting and not relaxed. With practice, you will start to realize and catch that feeling more quickly and stay grounded for longer. Use this and the other techniques I will show you in this book regularly to help ground yourself and hear what your intuition has to say.

For help with this exercise, download the free Groundedness Guided Visualization using the following link:

https://linktr.ee/kristenableson

Figure D

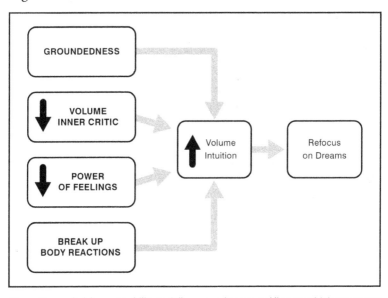

Figure D—maximizing your ability to follow your dreams and live your higher purpose involves being grounded, decreasing the volume of the Inner Critic, decreasing the power of feelings, and breaking up the body reactions.

What would happen if we stood on stage, had a very quiet Inner Critic, no thoughts of failing or doing it wrong, and no feelings of terror or anxiety instead of the inability to speak and a desire to get off stage before we had delivered a speech that would entice the audience to want to Step Up and be the people they were meant to be? What if it was a practice run and we missed cues, we laughed too loud, and we learned? And during all of this, our bodies were calm, our minds remained quiet, our feelings were light and full of joy and empowerment instead of fear and being bad, and we could hear the remarks from our higher self from our intuition as bright as day.

Throughout this book, I want to share with you the ways to decrease the volume of our Inner Critic, reduce the intensity of your feelings and their reactions, and break up all of those body patterns that keep you in your perfection pattern of behavior. These processes show you how to make it easier and fun to refocus on what you would truly love and be able to hear your intuition as though it is talking through a megaphone.

After all, the ultimate goal is to live your dreams and your higher purpose.

HOMEWORK

What Stepping Up activity have you done recently? It doesn't matter if you can't think of answers—it's just a way to get you to start being aware.

Part A

- What were you thinking?

- How were you feeling?

- What body reactions did you have?

- How did the answers to 1, 2, and 3 affect your outcome?

Do the imagination exercise on page 14: Set a timer for five minutes. After the timer goes off, think about the same Stepping Up activity in Part A of the first homework activity.

Part B

From your grounded space answer the following questions:

- What did I learn?

- What would I do differently next time?

- What resources do I need?

Use the information you have gained from this exercise to change future experiences.

To best assimilate the lessons you've just read and capture their full effect, please complete the homework before moving on to the next chapter.

2
INNER CRITIC

Don't speak negatively about yourself, even as a joke.
Your body doesn't know the difference. Words are
energy and cast spells, that's why it's called spelling.

—Bruce Lee

I recently watched a movie set in Australia in the 1950s. My thoughts went wild during one scene where a lady was going for a bushwalk with her new boyfriend.

That hair is well hair-sprayed. Interesting hairstyles for that era, but it would take too long to do, and it wouldn't be what you'd do for a bushwalk. It's actually over the top and has too much hair spray. What a waste of time. What a ridiculous thing to do. Great legs, though, but what fashion sense does that era have in shorts? Yikes. Very skinny legs. Yes, great for a girl. Shame I don't have that. She is pretty. Makeup's overdone, but I guess it's a movie; no one would do that normally. But yes, then there are those who wear full-face makeup to exercise here at the gym. Why do they do that? How ridiculous.

Note the constant dialogue and critique. And the rambling. Here, my mind is filled with everything I see, judging it according to the perfect aspect of it and, ultimately, of me. The Inner Critic is an attack on oneself by oneself. This can be experienced as being another voice—one outside of ourselves—but it is most definitely coming from within us.

Through consistent commenting and judging, the Inner Critic provides a running commentary on anything happening in our lives. It criticizes everything we think and do, comparing ourselves to perfection, and as we always fall short, its comments are always negative. Existence of the Inner Critic—to some extent—is in most people, but it's particularly active and hostile for perfectionists.

Looking back on my thoughts during the movie, I judged the hairstyle as overdone and, therefore, wrong. Maintaining the perfect hair in that situation required hairspray, but it also looked wrong. Consequently, it's wrong and not perfect. I then rated mine in comparison because everything I see is then related back to me. Considering my hair if I was walking in the bush, it would be a dismal failure. There's no way I could provide the perfect hairstyle to accommodate all the things one needs to look stunning in this situation—like the weather, wind, cold, and sweat. No, my hair would definitely fail in this situation. Hairspray may be the only thing that would keep it in the perfect place, but as I've decided, hairspray in this situation is wrong. My hair is obviously then a dismal failure. My hair is a waste of effort.

Note the exact judgment and the definite end of the argument.

In this dialogue explanation, you can see two things:

1) We use judging others as evidence to prove to ourselves without a doubt that we're not perfect and are, in fact, far from it.

2) We are constantly judging others.

Judgment as Evidence

The judgment is very matter of fact. We criticize everything according to what we feel is perfect. Our actions and behaviors are on show, and we judge ourselves, it seems, at every opportunity. Every detail—including details that really don't matter—are scrutinized. They are often focused on and made to be significant. Those minute details we ruminate over nail home the fact that there is evidence everywhere to reinforce that we're not perfect.

For some reason, it seems to be the only voice that we hear, listen to, and believe. We spend our days navigating the world with this internal judging voice that relentlessly criticizes, and we never seem to make headway towards our goal of perfection. The perfection model means that we continue to strive for such a thing in every moment, but as you can see, we never make it.

Our Inner Critic's attacks are always negative, as we always lack. They are personal and harsh. They hurt. In all honesty, because the Inner Critic is so loud and there's a lack of awareness, we don't realize our intuition exists and that there are other ideas out there.

It becomes the only opinion we hear, and so we believe it to be true. It's easy for us to critique; after all, we've been doing it since we were children. In fact, without any other knowledge, it feels like it's the only way; it comes so naturally we don't question it. It takes no effort and no time.

The consequence of pain is from continual self-hatred, self-judgment, and self-attack. Over time, as the Inner Critic is the only voice, we tend to hear the consequences; we start to feel more worthless, useless, hopeless, powerless, sad, depressed, and resentful. This can leave your body tense and defensive and can actually feel like you are physically attacking yourself. Of course, you aren't doing that, but the pain feels real.

According to our internal critic, nothing is good or positive, but awareness gives us the ability to start to learn and change what we hear and how we react. We need to make an effort to focus on the positive and see the scene through a more positive lens. Doing this takes effort as it's not our natural default, but it is possible. Noah Gershman sums this up effectively:

> The Inner Critic manifests as a disparaging internal voice that critiques and restricts one's thoughts, actions, and impulses. It makes demands for perfection in the uncompromising language of musts and shoulds and punishes any deviation or perceived failure with guilt, self-judgment, self-hatred, and shame.[3]

Judging Others

The movie set narrative is an example of how we attack others, but it's always about judging ourselves. We can come across quite nastily to others, often with epic sarcasm, a tirade of criticism, and passive aggression, but we don't aim to be nasty to others—it's all aimed at ourselves.

Our attack on others is a reflection of how imperfect we are ourselves—it's a sign of our Inner Critic being very harsh to us, and we are trying to feel less pain by doing either or both of two things:

1) Trying to protect ourselves from the hurt and pain by projecting it onto others to avoid the onslaught and pain ourselves, and

2) Merely trying to critique others to feel better about ourselves. If others aren't perfect and we see ourselves as better than them or not so hopeless and worthless, it hurts less.

The harshness of my critique of a person only reflects how harshly I'm judging myself. If I am more critical of myself, then my attack on a person can get worse. My remarks become curt and more direct, and I have less patience and acceptance. There's no directed malice to others—just towards ourselves.

A third way to reduce the pain that doesn't generally hurt others is to "numb out" or think of another place, perhaps where everything works out fine, we are perfect, and there's no pain. Numbing out is a total disconnection from your grounded space. I have treated many of these clients as a physiotherapist and also with the facilitation with horses. They aren't in their bodies at all and are very disconnected from their heart and higher self. (This can also be the result of trauma.)

When I was younger in primary school, I had to repeat my first year because I started too young. In the transition, I had no friends. To avoid the pain of self-critiquing, I would sit in the sun for the recess and lunchtimes and move my thoughts to another world. This enabled me to avoid the pain of the present moment and how hopeless I was, and it helped me endure that time of my life. As my Inner Critic worsened, I would often find myself in this paradigm. Life here didn't hurt, and everything was easy; everyone was lovely, and I was happy.

That coping mechanism wasn't a healthy option and certainly isn't an effective way to ground yourself and connect to your higher purpose and intuition. It moves you further away from being grounded altogether. If you keep listening to the Inner Critic, you will continue to hear its critiques and react in a way you always have.

As a perfectionist, if you find yourself acting this way towards others, then this awareness tells you at this very moment you are judging and attacking yourself horribly. In my experience, I can feel extremely useless, powerless, and worthless. I'm projecting onto others and can be more sarcastic—this unconsciously feels like it may hurt less. But it doesn't. We need to step out of this pattern, learn to ground ourselves, and eventually love ourselves. Only then can we attempt to refocus and hear our intuitive guidance.

Inner Critic's Constant Chatter

The constant chatter of the Inner Critic worsens in a conversation; the Inner Critic's judgments and discrepancies can become harsher for any number of reasons, but they're most evident in environments where we need to be seen as perfect.

In conversation with others, many thoughts arise: Should I know what the conversation is about? What will I say? How long should I talk? Have I spoken for too long? Was that funny enough?

The Inner Critic evaluates everything to decide how I am doing by constantly navigating other reactions and judging how I am doing according to them.

With others, there are now more opinions, more to be aware of and control, and thus, there's more to react to. *How do I behave, and what do I have to say to maintain the perfect conversation?* I need to monitor all moods and reactions and respond accordingly. I need to act perfectly, listen completely, and add the perfect amount of conversation in the perfect timing, with the ideal humor if required, but not talk for too long without upsetting anyone. And definitely not cause any conflict. Additionally, I have to be able to read everyone's different personalities and moods at that particular moment to add what is required to avoid conflict and act perfectly with no emotion for every conversation, environment, and relationship. Well, it's impossible, and it's also exhausting. The Inner Critic, with time, gets louder and harsher.

My Inner Critic monitors my thoughts, what I say, and how I say it, and it attacks all of it.

On top of that, it adds comments on how it thinks others perceive me—and it's never positive. Even if I feel good about something, it will find the smallest and often irrelevant detail that was imperfect and make it the only thing that mattered. It will focus on this detail and make it bigger until that's all I remember about the conversation. Hence, also attacking, never positive, never joyful, consistently wrong, and always imperfect. For example, a situation could be that people laughed at what I said but the conversation stopped after I spoke. My Inner Critic has focused on this aspect and decided that this is bad, that the lack of conversation is my fault, that what I said was actually not funny, not coherent, no interesting, and irrelevant.

So, how do we stop listening to this Inner Critic or lessen the effect it has on us?

Firstly, we need to acknowledge it affects us. This act takes some of the intensity out of its tirade.

- In the words of Byron Katie in 2017, ask yourself the following questions:
  o Is it true?
  o Can you absolutely know that it's true?
  o How do you react when you believe that thought?
  o Who would you be without the thought?[4]

It still is difficult, however, to refocus away from the Inner Critic. Often, when we are in the thick of it, we can't see another way. This can be quite destructive.

In the clutches of it, all that's possible is being aware you're in the grips of the patterns. Still, those tentacles are strong. The Inner Critic's screams are so loud that you can't hear anything else, let alone the strong, quiet voice of your higher purpose saying to be calm and breathe. When the screaming is there, it's hard to focus on something else, especially when that something else is so quiet.

What we need and would love is for this Inner Critic to be less impactful and less influential. To be less in volume so we can hear other things, and it doesn't take over our lives, to connect to what really matters and enjoy what's around us without the inner voice that's constantly commenting and growing louder.

When we can take the volume and power out of our Inner Critic, then our true empowerment begins. We're no longer a slave to its whims or react to what it says. This is when we can ground ourselves and connect fully to our higher purpose and follow the path of our intuition.

I See Me

Often, we are so stuck in our reactions and thoughts that it becomes almost impossible to get out of them and see things from a different point of view. This technique enables just that. Acknowledging where you're at and changing focus isn't enough. You need more, something substantial to pull you out of that energy and away from the voice of the Inner Critic. This will give you a chance to refocus and make different decisions.

The process starts by imagining you are outside of yourself—simply imagine you're looking at your physical self at that moment from a distance. Take a good look at the figure (you) you see. How do you look? What's your posture? How's your thinking making you act? How are you reacting to life and to others? Why are life and others responding to you like they are?

This technique is helpful when you are in your reactions and so deeply connected to your emotions that you can't step out of the response. That is when you're in the grips of needing to be perfect, needing to be correct, and unable to get out of the pain, when your head is pounding from the voice of the Inner Critic, and you just can't think. With this technique, you can look at yourself from afar and really see your physical form of who you have become when you are heavily in these reactions, processes, and thoughts. This enables you to see the effects of your reactions: how you react to people, what your posture is, and how people react to you. You could look at your facial expression and your mind overthinking things and see why people were reacting to you the way they are and why you were reacting to situations and people the way you were. From this space, you are outside of the intensity of the reaction, which enables you to ground yourself more easily and breathe. It allows you to see the bigger picture and make different decisions.

So, by looking from a few meters away, you help yourself in many ways:

- Getting some clarity
    - o An insight into how you are in the world
    - o Being aware of how your patterns play out
    - o How you look and act when you think and feel this way
    - o What you look like to others, why others may react to you in specific ways, and why you are responding to them in certain ways—why you are reacting or being triggered

- A way of escaping the intense energy of your habits, patterns, and beliefs so you can see things from a different perspective

- A way of grounding yourself, calming yourself down, and giving yourself the ability to react differently to the situation

- Changing your posture, relaxing your tenseness, and reacting how you would like to instead of how your patterns propel you to

- Giving yourself a virtual cuddle, some love, compassion, help, and support—self-love instead of self-hatred and berating

- A place to step outside the mind

With practice, it can help you be quicker at making better decisions.

This can help to pull away for enough time to change your thinking towards a different viewpoint. You can surrender, let go, and react differently (see later chapters). In this space, you're more able to get out of the vice of the pattern and can finally start to gain some awareness about how and why you react to others and why they react to you.

This technique requires practice. With all techniques, you need to practice them throughout the day, so when you are heavy in your pattern, it's easier to remember to use this.

HOMEWORK

Become aware of a recent experience or scene where you are commenting to yourself or others. What is happening to you?

Part A

- What are you saying? What are you feeling?

- What are you telling yourself? What action(s) are you taking? Is your body reacting? (This could be anything—don't overthink this, just write down the first things that come to mind.)

- Close your eyes (only if it is safe to do so).

- Imagine looking at yourself from a few meters away.

- Continue to breathe and just observe.

- What do you see? What is your posture? How are you acting?

- Notice how your thinking and acting affect your actions. How are you reacting to life, to others, and why are life and others responding to you like that?

- Continue to breathe.

- Ground yourself and continue to observe.

- Give yourself some love and compassion—physically hug yourself if that feels appropriate.

Part B

- Come back into your body and notice the difference.

- Continue to stay in this more grounded space and take notice: How else could you react in this situation that would not be from your thoughts, Inner Critic, feelings, and body reactions? From this space, your grounded self, what action could you take that would benefit you? Your higher purpose? The person you want to be?

- How can you change your posture to help with this process? Take as long as you like with this.

- What are you learning about yourself? How could you have reacted differently to the original scenario? What could be the possible consequences of these different reactions?

- How can this awareness help you when you're in this situation or experience again?

You could also try this when in conversation with others and you are struggling to stay present.

This tool is effective in helping you get out of your own way. It makes it easier to lessen the grip your Inner Critic and body reactions have on you. The more you can reduce their impact, the more grounded the decisions you can start to make.

To best assimilate the lessons you've just read and capture their full effect, please complete the homework before moving on to the next chapter.

3

CONSEQUENCES OF THE HARSH INNER CRITIC

Rather than being your thoughts and emotions,
be the awareness behind them

—Eckhart Tolle

As we have established, the Inner Critic's voice is often the only voice we pay attention to. It seems to fill our heads and can be very loud. In this space, you can't hear anything else. There's no room for anything else. Several consequences arise as a result:

COMMUNICATION BECOMES DIFFICULT.

You often can't hear other people, let alone your other thoughts.

- It's not that your ears stop working; it's just the noise from the Inner Critic is so loud it makes it difficult to hear anything else. There's no capacity for any other thought. For me, people often sound muffled, like they are underwater. It seems like they are in a haze or are distant, and I can't quite hear them or understand what they are saying.

- There's no space to hear anything else, so my higher purpose and intuition are also challenging to hear.

It's hard to take in information, especially when there is no chance to think about it, discuss it, understand it, and process it. Processing information that people say to you and having scope in your mind to think it over becomes challenging.

When the noise is loud, and we can't hear ourselves think, speaking can become difficult. *What do I say next? How do I formulate the answers if I can't hear the words I want to say?* Perfectionists, in general, will often try to talk with very controlled words and phrases, trying to find the perfect way to express themselves. Often, speaking becomes jerky or shaky as words are challenging to find. People often want to finish your sentences for you as you can't quite find the words or aren't fast enough to do it yourself. Over time, the words are harder to find, and conversation flows less easily.

DECREASED LEARNING, FOCUS ABILITY AND MEMORY

I love to learn. Without fail, though, while I'm in a course or lecture, within a short amount of time, I just want to leave. The initial part is usually fabulous—it's all new and fascinating, and I'm keeping up with others. I love what I hear.

My Internal Critic soon starts to increase its critique: I'm not learning as fast as others, how stupid am I, and so forth, increasing in volume until that voice is all I can hear. It focuses on everything except what the facilitator is saying. I can't hear the message they are delivering.

It doesn't take long for our focus to wane and for us to become distracted. It isn't because we aren't interested; it's because our Inner Critic's comments have taken over.

- Its volume is loud, and it's hard to stay focused on what someone else is saying.

- It focuses on minor, negative, often irrelevant details like "the facilitator's smile is weird" and "what an outfit." These elements become the focus rather than what they are saying.

- If I can't take the information in, there's no space to process it, making it difficult to learn and, therefore, difficult to remember. For me, I remember what I think about; if I only hear my inabilities and focus on the outfit the facilitator is wearing, then that's what I will remember.

The booming noise of the Inner Critic is so distracting that it becomes difficult to listen and hear the quieter tones of the higher purpose and intuition. When a megaphone continuously erupts in your ear, it becomes difficult not to listen to it when the alternative—intuition—is a quiet calm.

EXHAUSTION

The more the Inner Critic talks, the more my body reacts; the anxiety grows, pain starts, my body gets tight, and the focus wanes. To focus and listen and maintain that mask of perfection takes extra strength and thus extra control. Simply put, the mind that overworks and analyzes as much as the perfectionist's mind does can lead to physical, emotional, and mental exhaustion. There's no space for peace.

PHYSICAL PAIN

An active, overreacting, and debilitating Inner Critic can cause physical pain as an increase in self-abuse and body reactions hurt.

Our body reactions include physical body pain, migraines, stiffness, and eyestrain. To avoid the pain, we can distract, disconnect, or move our attention to a fantasy world where life is peaceful and perfect.

With a constant attack on ourselves, we internalize self-hatred and anger, which can lead to sadness, depression, and chronic illness. Our self-esteem is low, and our boundaries are almost non-existent as we view ourselves as wrong compared to everyone else.

IT'S HARD TO SEE THE POSITIVES

With constant focus on imperfections, flaws, details, and negatives, it isn't easy to see the positives. When we recall a situation or a story, we tend to focus on what we remember, thought, felt, and what we've said—it's usually negative. Unless we start to be aware and teach ourselves to see the positive, to focus on what we did well, and not be distracted by irrelevant details, this perfectionist pattern will not change.

For example, when watching the movie, I became transfixed on the hairstyle of the main actress in the film, missing the depth of emotion she was portraying. Instead, I noticed every aspect of the set: the clothes, the actors' hair, their acting ability, facial expressions, height, shoes, and everything in between. It can be difficult to let go of the control and allow a story to take me where the director wants me to go. When I focus on details, it becomes nearly impossible to simply enjoy the character development and the plot of a story.

EFFECTS OF OTHERS' ATTACKS

You can never say anything worse to me that I don't already say to myself.

Others' comments on anything we do or say can feel like an attack. It may not be meant as anything—just a simple passing comment—but our mind sees it as an attack as our degree of self-abuse is already quite high. So, it doesn't take much for others to put us over the edge—and it can be something basic like a comment or opinion. We take it personally and find it hard to laugh at our imperfections and mistakes. Anger, rage, depression, sadness, confusion, and passive aggression are common reactions.

We are trying very hard to hold it together, control everything, and maintain that mask of perfection. Even with awareness, it's hard to receive critique from others and even laugh with them. It's our greatest battle—to laugh at ourselves, let go of control, and be imperfect. Laughing means we are comfortable with all the things we are striving to avoid—our imperfections and wrongness.

Matthew Ignoffo, a teacher of English composition, literature, and remedial reading, conveys when he started to teach remedial reading to disadvantaged college prep readers how difficult it was to teach when the Inner Critic had so much negative influence over their thoughts and behaviors. He goes on to say how, for his own career, he needed to overcome and free himself from his Inner Critic and its way of power, control, and sabotage.

When attempting to teach remedial reading, he made an observation:

> I suspected that no matter what I proposed to them, their negative 'Inner Critic' voices would tell them "it's useless—you're as good as you will ever be now. Why bother to work?" I myself was a remedial reader in high school and heard the convincing defeatist voice telling

me I would know perpetual academic defeat brought about by my hopeless dislike of reading and helpless fear of failure. It was only when I consciously began to free myself of my own Inner Critic that I was able to overcome self-sabotaging academic behavior. [5]

How to Reduce the Volume and Effect of Our Inner Critic

Breathing

Whether you like it or not, what you think, feel, and tell yourself affects the health of your immune system, stress, and anxiety levels. Controlled breathing enables you to get out of your head, ground yourself, and refocus. Long-term benefits increase awareness and mindfulness and reduce stress.

Unless addressed, chronic stress has many severe consequences for your health. The stress response keeps the body's nervous system on high alert by releasing cortisol, causing our minds to remain overactive and greatly affecting the immune response. Chronic heightened blood pressure and heart rates have their own effects—increased chances of strokes and injuries, not to mention lack of sleep.

Controlled breathing exercises can help lower your blood pressure, promote feelings of calm and relaxation, and relieve stress. It activates the calming side of the nervous system, telling your body all is safe and well. It activates your para-sympathetic nervous system, whose job is to balance out the effects of the fight or flight reaction. The more we practice controlled breathing exercises, the more the body will understand that we want the body to work in this calmer way all the time. You can teach it to function more efficiently by practicing these exercises regularly.

When you first start practicing this exercise, it is helpful to be in a space where there are no distractions, and you can focus easily. By making this practice a daily task, you can start to see the benefits of clearer focus, improved memory, reduced anxiety, and maintaining calm and clarity.

Once you understand the process, you can take it with you into your day drawing on it whenever you feel it will help you connect.

There are many types of breathing regimens. This one is simple, reproducible, and effective.

(If you have breathing issues or lung problems, you may need to consult your doctor or physiotherapist to adapt this exercise for you.)

1) Sitting comfortably, bring your attention to your breath.

2) Breathe in through your nose and out through your mouth.

3) Place your hands on your sides at the bottom of your ribcage.

4) Imagine your chest is a flask. Take a normal breath in so that you fill the bottom of the flask first (not a deep breath).

5) When you do this, you will feel your bottom ribs move out under your hands when you inhale and move in when you exhale.

6) Be aware of shallow breathing—this is where you breathe into your upper chest. Your shoulders may shrug up with this technique. This form of breathing is what people mostly use when they are stressed or anxious. Try to be aware of this and immediately bring your attention down to the bottom of your lungs and ribs again.

7) You want to breathe in for four to six counts, hold it for four to six counts, and release it for another four to six counts.

8) Repeat this process. I would suggest a minimum of five to ten times to start getting some effect. More repetitions give a greater effect. Consider doing this practice daily, starting for ten minutes at a time and working up to thirty minutes.

Regularly repeating this simple technique helps make it easy to remember, especially when you're at the height of anxiety or stress. Remember to relax your shoulders and bring your attention to your body and breath.

I've had patients this has benefitted. One was at college studying beauty therapy. She had issues with a loud Inner Critic and, when focusing on reading material in practical sessions, became more stressed and panicked. She was unable to concentrate and, therefore, unable to complete tasks. She seemed destined to fail. I taught her the above breathing technique. Within a few weeks of practicing this technique and doing it while taking her practical examination, she was able to focus, follow through, and complete the task successfully. It's a powerful technique.

Meditation

Research findings support meditation as a crucial part of a healthy body and mind. It is a beautiful way to calm the mind and thus calm the body. Meditation is a mind and body practice. The National Center for Complementary and Integrative Health claims this about the practice:

Meditation has a long history of use for increasing calmness and physical relaxation, improving psychological balance, coping with illness, and enhancing overall health and well-being.

Mind and body practices focus on the interactions among the brain, mind, body, and behavior.

There are many types of meditation, but most have four elements in common: a quiet location with as few distractions as possible, a specific and comfortable posture (sitting, lying down, walking, or other positions), a focus of attention (a specially chosen word or set of words, an object, or the sensations of the breath), and an open attitude (letting distractions come and go naturally without judging them).[6]

An interesting thing to remember when a perfectionist first starts to meditate is the thoughts can be overwhelming. Up to this time, we have controlled them and not allowed ourselves to hear all of them. There are so many thoughts. We often dissociate from all of the thoughts, so suddenly hearing them at once can be quite intense. This passes as the practice continues, but it's nice to be aware of it at the start. So, keep going.

I try three forms of meditation: one focuses on my breathing, another with my eyes open and focusing on an object (an object from nature works better), and the last with the Ho'oponopono prayer.

1) Sit in a quiet space and close your eyes. If closing your eyes feels unsafe for any reason, then keep your eyes open. Start to bring your attention to your breath. Begin the breathing regimen (described in the breathing section above). Breathe in for four to six counts, hold for four to six counts, and breath out for four to six counts. Repeat.

Once you're in a rhythm, it becomes easier. Be aware of your thoughts as they flow in but don't grab onto any and ponder them. Simply acknowledge them and let them go. I suggest you set a timer for ten minutes to start with and stay there for the entire ten minutes. Your mind will want to stop and will give you all kinds of reasons to do so. Stay there for the time you have allocated. Try to do this daily. It works better if you do it at a similar time and in a similar space.

2) As I am easily distracted when my eyes are open, I find the second mediation works well for me. I simply find something natural like a leaf, find a quiet spot, and sit. I calm my breath and keep my eyes focused on the object—the leaf, in this case—being aware of my thoughts and not letting them ponder what I am looking at. Again, I just want to look and notice. What generally happens is the detail of the leaf will become more visible, and then you will see even more detail.

Again, set a timer and continue until the timer goes off. Stay on the same timer setting for a week, then gradually increase. Try to do this practice daily. This meditation was originally done with a rose I found in the book *The Monk Who Sold His Ferrari* by Robin Sharma.[7]

3) Meditation + the Ho'oponopono prayer (see Chapter 4 for complete explanation) is a technique that helps you focus on any feeling you are sitting in or thought or resistance you're noticing. Simply repeat the prayer. The meditative works are calming, and the prayer gradually reduces the resistance, making the feeling more manageable.

HOMEWORK

Part A

- Find a space where you cannot be disturbed.

- Sit comfortably and close your eyes (only if safe to do so).

- Notice your thoughts and feelings. Allow them to be there.

- Give your overall state of stress a number from 0–10 (Zero being no stress, ten being fully stressed). This number will change over time as you become more aware of your resting stress state. Initially, as perfectionists are so used to stress feeling normal, you may feel this as strange and not understand its relevance. Keep checking this number over time and see if it changes.

- Set a timer for five minutes (You can always do longer—there is no maximum time limit).

- Place hands on the outside of your lower ribs.

- Feel the ribs move out against your hands as you breathe in, feel them move in as you breathe out. Bring your attention to your hands on your ribs and how they are moving. Feel and concentrate on your hands as you breathe in and out. You can also imagine air moving into your lungs and out again. Remember, it's important to send air down to the bottom of your lungs. Take normal breaths, not deep ones—the difference is you are sending the air to the lower part of the lungs first. If you maintain the breathing and focus without your hands on your ribs, lower your hands to your sides. If you like the feedback your hands on the ribs give you, then continue as is.

- Breathe in for four counts, hold for four counts, breathe out to the count of four. You can extend this count to five or six if you feel comfortable doing so.

- Repeat until the timer goes off.

Part B

- In this new space, notice your thoughts and feelings; notice how your body is. Does anything feel different from before? Assess again your overall state of stress (numbered from 0–10).

- Repeat the above with your eyes open.

When next you find yourself in a situation where you have problems concentrating, try this technique. Notice how your body changes.

To best assimilate the lessons you've just read and capture their full effect, please complete the homework before moving on to the next chapter.

4

ANXIETY/FEELING OVERWHELMED

Anxiety (about/over something) —the state of feeling nervous or worried that something bad is going to happen.

—Oxford Dictionary

Anxiety can be normal in stressful situations such as public speaking or taking a test. Anxiety is only an indicator of underlying disease when feelings become excessive, all-consuming, and interfere with daily living.

—Mayo Clinic

Common anxiety signs and symptoms include the following:

- Feeling nervous, restless, or tense
- Having a sense of impending danger, panic, or doom
- Having an increased heart rate
- Breathing rapidly (hyperventilation)

- Sweating

- Trembling

- Feeling weak or tired

- Trouble concentrating or thinking about anything other than the present worry

- Having trouble sleeping

- Experiencing gastrointestinal (GI) problems

- Having difficulty controlling worry

- Having the urge to avoid things that trigger anxiety

Chronic anxiety is a crippling feeling that can stop people in their tracks. It's a body reaction that can be so powerful it renders the person unable to speak, function, perform, show up, or get up. Anxiety and stress have been heightened in recent times and are a symptom of most clients I see.

The depth of anxiety can change according to the person, task, situation, and the factors in life. People deal with anxiety differently, and there are many factors and causes, but it affects most people in varying degrees.

Anxiety can render you frozen and unable to move or think how to move. It's unreasonable to believe that anxiety is a fleeting thing; it tends to flow in waves and can last varying lengths of time. The result is that tasks are not completed with ease or at all. The path forward, if it moves forward, is jerky.

In my experience, anxiety affect my behavior and ability to move forward. My perfectionism is the root of much of the anxiety I deal with. When a wave of anxiety hits, nothing is in focus or comes together as I would wish. Feeling overwhelmed, I freeze; it affects my breathing and my ability to think clearly or logically. I don't seem to be able to start the task, finish the task, or do anything in between. Even attempting to break the task into small fragments causes me to be overwhelmed as

I question whether the pieces are correct or if I will do them in the right order. I become unable to focus, stunned, like a deer caught in the headlights of a car.

Anxiety isn't something that we wake up with someday. It's often been impacting us for years. If we don't find strategies to deal with this, then there are consequences as we get older. It's helpful to find the cause and triggers.

Anxiety symptoms are extremely common in childhood and adolescence and can negatively interfere with general well-being, social life, academic performance, and development of social skills. Anxiety symptoms are associated with impairment of memory and cognitive functions and can contribute to poor school performance and academic failure, which can, in turn, lead to further psychiatric disturbances.

It is something you sense in your body—it is your body's reaction to your thoughts and feelings. When you are in a state of anxiety, it's difficult to snap out of that space, start to problem solve it, and change it to attempt to improve your function.

There are many reasons for anxiety. As a perfectionist, my anxiety increases the longer I put off something that has to be done. It's beneficial to sit with things and think them through until that aha moment arrives or you can see things clearer. But when the feeling of anxiety is overwhelming, or I feel it starting to increase, it's helpful to get clear on some sort of action. To realize what's causing the anxiety is a step forward in battling the problem and breaking it down so we can find some relief. Often, I feel anxious, and I don't know why. Lack of decision-making is one example that causes anxiety for me being a perfectionist, hence putting off something that needs to be done.

To overcome it, I look at what I'm doing. Is there a decision I need to make? There's no way this exhausts the list for reasons that anxiety occurs, but it has been helpful for me when I feel anxious to look for a decision I've been putting off attempting to deal with. I then review how I feel once a decision has been made, no matter how big or small. That's the point when the anxiety feeling can often be relieved. It may be as big as confronting someone about a conflict or whether to get out of bed now or later. This sounds so easy, and often you know exactly what you need to do. You just can't do it. It becomes quite an amazing symptom of procrastination, making it harder to start the task as well as a cause.

SHORT-TERM HELP

The following are techniques that I have discovered and have used over the years that help me snap out of a frozen space or anxiety where I can't seem to focus or function. As I have mentioned before, when you are in the thick of this anxiety space, it's difficult to remember or see anything else. With practice, it gets easier to remember what these techniques are and so becomes quicker to act on their helpful ways. I have found that the speed at which you can refocus and thus move forward may be faster if you practice these techniques. This being said, the anxiety and space still occur with the same triggers—this doesn't really change, hence *short-term* help.

Eye for Detail

Years ago, when I looked after a young filly, she reminded me to refocus my attention to detail. I learned a method to help refocus in times of anxiety; you focus on the five senses—try to smell, touch, see, hear, and taste. I always found this too much to remember when I was anxious. She taught me a different way. She encouraged me to look at a leaf or a flower, just one, something small in the landscape and to simply focus on it. If you are not in nature, then you can find any object in the scene around you, something simple that doesn't have writing on it. For example, a pen. When I was with her, I was in nature, and it was easy for me to find a leaf or small branch. So, I turned to the nearest leaf and began to focus on it. By focusing on it, you start to see it in more detail. The leaf starts to express a variety of branches, veins, and colors. As you look for longer, the detail starts to unfold with thickness and lines that you hadn't seen when you first spied it.

By focusing on the detail of one thing and not allowing your focus to deviate, you can move your attention from frozen and unable to function to being able to function, moving out of that anxiety reaction.

The steps to unfreeze yourself from anxiety are simple:

1) Look around and spy an object.

2) Keep looking at it—don't let your mind take you anywhere else.

3) Notice it, start to breathe, notice the detail, and keep focused on the detail.

4) Notice more detail and keep breathing.

5) When you feel like your body is calmer and your eyes and mind aren't darting everywhere, you can review the task at hand.

Do Something Physical

Physically moving can help shake up the energy in your body. It can make it easier to break up the frozen sense and move forward both mentally and physically. Often, going for a walk or doing something different like squats or star jumps on the spot can help to reset and refocus.

LONG-TERM HELP

Long-term help is different from short-term help as when used, this technique helps not only to decrease the anxiety at the time of its use, but its intensity seems reduced for good. Over time, when applied to the same anxieties and triggers, the same trigger causes little or much less anxiety, allowing it to be easier for us to function and focus. I love this technique. It has truly changed my life.

Ho'oponopono Prayer—An ancient Hawaiian Meditation

Ho'oponopono prayer is an ancient Hawaiian practice for forgiveness and reconciliation. It's way more than a prayer, though.

I came across this years ago as a way to reduce the power of the patterns in my body and to calm my body. It's a long-term use, because when you use it, the intensity of the pattern goes forever. It seems to have a permanent effect on the feeling or situation you're focusing on when performing the prayer.

Jennifer Williamson writes, "It's the act and intention of holding space for reflection, repentance, forgiveness, and gratitude. She further states, "The Philosophy behind this practice is that we're each responsible for what shows up in our reality. We own our feelings and our experiences. So even if someone else has wronged us, we're the ones saying the prayer."[8]

I may have lost some of you with this, thinking it's a bunch of hippy nonsense. But let me tell you, it works. And in combination with other things (like meditation or breathing), it's a powerful tool to reduce the power of your patterns, reduce your reactions, calm yourself, and ground. If nothing else, it places you into a lovely meditative space out of your head and into your body.

What I love about this meditation is that you can do it anywhere and at any time. Simply, if you're feeling any reaction like someone is annoying you, you have a lot of emotion, or an active Inner Critic is crowding your thoughts, you will love this meditation. Here is the mantra:

I'm sorry
Please forgive me
Thank you
I love you

That's it! You simply say it over and over again. The results are phenomenal—your reactions calm down and stay that way. The next time you are triggered, your reaction is less. You will see things more clearly and be able to relax. It actually reduces the response, so you're not so triggered the next time.

It's great to combine this with breathing into your body or being mindful of air going into the bottom of your lungs and slowing your breathing down. It's a bit difficult to count out the breaths, so just keep repeating the phrase instead.

You don't need to sit cross-legged to do this. I've done this while doing a whole range of activities—while in meetings, listening to or giving tutorials, and even while talking to others. I love the meditative effect it has on my mind and my body; it's transportable, and no one can see you are using it.

What's more, it's effective—it helps you heal your thoughts, past, and patterns.

HOMEWORK

Practice the *Ho'oponopono* prayer.

Part A

- Find a space where you won't be disturbed.

- Sit or lay comfortably.

- Choose to have your eyes opened or closed (only close your eyes if safe to do so).

- Notice your anxiety levels and other thoughts and feelings and allow them to be there.

- Give your overall anxiety or emotional state a number from 0–10 (Zero being nothing, ten being fully anxious).

- Begin to say the phrase out loud or to yourself over and over again.

  - I'm sorry

  - Please forgive me

  - Thank you

  - I love you

- Repeat the phrase until the level of anxiety or emotion reduces to around two or three out of ten.

Part B

- Remember a recent time when you were anxious. If it is safe to do so, sit in those feelings and anxiety you had then. Assign your anxiety level a number out of ten.

- Repeat the phrase above. Notice after doing this that it is easier to ground yourself, quiet your Inner Critic and body reactions—like anxiety—and follow your intuition.

- As mentioned in Chapter 3, the *Ho'oponopono* prayer can also be used with meditation.

It's also important to remember that we have dreams, and this is a part of us. If you are finding the material overwhelming, then do the techniques to reduce the overwhelm. Breathe.

Never underestimate the art of journaling. It can be an effective tool to use daily and enables you to remove some clutter from your mind and help your clarity become more obvious. It helps to find that intuitive voice and to increase its volume.

To help find your purpose, you can use journaling. Simply find a space where you are not going to be disturbed and ground yourself using one of the techniques you have practiced so far.

Sit in this space and, while grounded, write whatever comes to you. Don't worry about getting it perfect or if you don't understand—just try. The more we practice the techniques and listen for our intuition, the more clarity we gain around it.

To best assimilate the lessons you've just read and capture their full effect, please complete the homework before moving on to the next chapter.

5

ACCOMPLISHING A TASK

Procrastination makes easy things hard, hard things harder.

—Mason Cooley

A perfectionist may find it difficult to complete tasks for any number of reasons, and at the root of all of those excuses and delays, of course, is the fear of not doing the task perfectly. Why do we procrastinate? What are some of the reasons behind not completing or at the other end of the scale not knowing when to stop? Is there a balance?

PROCRASTINATION

"I just can't start . . ."

I used to have a tutor in school to help me with essay writing. I would get the topic of the essay, think of a great introduction, and imagine how it would flow. I would like it, be happy with it, try to write it, and it was gone. I couldn't remember how it started—and it had to start that way—so I couldn't start. I would ponder something else, some other tact, and the same thing would happen. I would see how it flowed, liked the angle where it would take me, would try to write it, but I'd forget the exact wording to start it. *Can't start. Try again.*

This is how I used to approach anything. I needed to see it to the end, but I could never really remember how it started. If I couldn't remember how it began, then it could go down a different path—one I couldn't foresee. That was too risky, so I didn't start. I remember my tutor saying to me, "Just start." I would look at her strangely and wince. I couldn't, couldn't she see?

If I start and it goes down a different or incorrect path, then I could fail. I needed to know it was going to flow where I wanted the storyline to go. To achieve this, I had to remember exactly how it started. Only then would it finish the way I foresaw.

AVOIDANCE

Avoiding potential failure increases levels of anxiety and tension. Often, perfectionists have a task or project, and we find anything to do except that. We waste a lot of time achieving nothing or focusing on tasks that aren't a priority instead of doing the job we need to do, like surveying the fridge again for food—even though things haven't changed—or cleaning the house. The anxiety increases, and procrastination sets in.

Perfectionists like certainty. We want to know the path we take won't fail. If procedures follow black and white rules, it's easier to navigate, but when we need to consider others or other changing factors, we can never be sure. We like to know the path and the end and how it all will look. Surprises or tangents are not preferred as we haven't considered them, and they could be wrong.

It can be a series of decisions. We often just need to make a decision and start.

The longer we leave the decision, the more resistance builds up, the more we churn on making the decision, and the more anxiety and tension we feel. All of this also makes it harder and harder to start. To avoid feeling the tension, we procrastinate. This can include numbing out or doing other, easier things we know, such as cleaning the fridge, sleeping, and general avoidance.

By the time you finally start the task or make the decision, the tension is palpable, but the relief is instant. You also wonder why you didn't start this earlier and did this to yourself yet again. Next time this happens, try and remember how it felt to start. Start being aware.

It's interesting to note here that perfectionists liken too many inputs to chaos. They find it much easier to follow a set of rules. There can be too many options to consider with chaos, and the right and correct way is challenging to find.

LEAVING THE TASK TO THE LAST MINUTE

Though the reactions of anxiety can be similar, the experience is different. Avoiding starting often means you try but can't start. You look busy but get nothing done.

Leaving the job to the last minute means you let it go and don't consider it until the last minute. It's in the back of your head, but you don't get around to it. Some people love the adrenaline of the limited timeline, which helps push them through to the deadline and through the impending anxiety.

It's like the "unable to start" scenario because this also avoids the anxiety, self-criticism, and potential failure that always arises. With a deadline, we have less time to feel these reactions. It also enables us to blame our inadequate performance on something seemingly out of our control, such as lack of sleep, coffee, or the lack of ink in the printer. It permits us to be mediocre and to be ok with that. You can live with yourself because it wasn't entirely your fault. The Inner Critic will attack you less.

The disadvantage of procrastinating and leaving things to the last minute is that people—and often you—have no idea what you are truly capable of doing. You disappoint yourself and lessen your self-respect.

As we are fully aware, when we start a task, the Inner Critic's critiques will start—let the judgments begin! As we continue, so does the Inner Critic, and that's often less than pleasant. The continual repercussions of continuing a task are overanalysis, potential stress, and exhaustion. Things that aren't that comfortable are avoided.

NEEDING TO TWEAK: FINDING BALANCE

Some perfectionists will try to get a task done perfectly and churn over it despite it being excellent by anyone else's standards. They will change the already finished document many times and will never be happy with what they hand over. Ever. Something always needs to be changed. It's never perfect.

I have a friend who told me about her colleague who is a perfectionist. That person will remain behind for hours after everyone else has gone home just to add final touches to a room. She has to make sure everything is perfect by her standards. This is fine; however, there's a line where the room was perfectly adequate for the task. Tweaking it didn't gain much effect, so the time and effort put in was unnecessary. It's hard to find and be happy with that mindset.

Perfectionists can waste much valuable time and effort staying late to finish the final touches on something that was sufficient many hours before. In this situation, the task can never really be done. There's always something to change. It torments the perfectionist. It's hard to draw the line and accept the job is done. To the perfectionist, it never feels complete. Other perfectionists leave tasks not quite finished by choice, or the job done is half-hearted. This is often a consequence of avoiding the tweaking process.

As we live in a world where projects need to be completed and assignments need to be handed in, it's easier to make an average attempt than try to be perfect and never finish. Some learn they can never do it perfectly, so why try? Allowing yourself to reach that point where you're trying to be perfect and know you'll fail is often far more painful than not trying at all. Yes, the job is done; it's just not done to the best of your ability. The line between the satisfaction of doing a great job and that continual need to be perfect is difficult to see. Sometimes, it's less painful to make a half-hearted effort than to end up doing the endless further tweaks needed and fall into a heap from exhaustion.

The lesser of two evils can be the average attempt at a task because it becomes a better outcome than the perfect attempt, the never knowing when to pull out and never succeeding. Both are painful. Our behavior usually follows the one that is least painful. Procrastination is powerfully destructive for getting a task done or making decisions. There is always potential burnout from increased stress or an inability to stop tweaking and find balance.

SHORT-TERM SOLUTIONS

Make the decision.

If you are aware of the rising anxiety, tension, or other emotions like passive aggression or reduced patience and the ongoing irritability you may feel when you need to make a decision, then ask yourself what decision, large or small, you're avoiding. Often, you aren't aware that this is the reason you're procrastinating. Once you locate the decision to be made, then, in my experience, you can begin to reduce the tension. It's even better if you can make the decision. This may lead to other decisions and unknowns, which might be why you procrastinate, but once you start the decision-making process, the resistance often reduces, and the path becomes clearer.

Chunk down the task.

The task can be very overwhelming if you view it as one whole. Breaking down the task into bite-size pieces can reduce the anxiety and overwhelming sensations and help complete the task. Break down the task and place the chunks in order of priority.

Do one thing.

Doing only one thing is a common piece of advice from many successful businesspeople. Notably, the book *Do One Thing* by Gary W. Keller and Jay Papasan offers practical advice and reasoning for the process.

Complete.

Doing one thing from the chunking it down process enables you to complete a task. It's difficult as a perfectionist to complete something if we constantly feel we need to tweak it. Making things tangible makes this easier.

Celebrate the wins.

Once completed, no matter how insignificant the Inner Critic makes your completion seem, it's important to celebrate. This helps finalize the process and enables you to channel the momentum into the next project or task. If we don't celebrate or acknowledge our completions, then there are many open-ended tasks that our thoughts return to, scattering our energy and focus and lessening our ability to create momentum.

Just do something.

Start doing something and adjust as you go. If you're having trouble with starting, then just put pen to paper. You'll be amazed how quickly a path becomes available for you to follow. The Inner Critic doesn't tell you that the path is never set in stone. So whatever direction you start, there's always room to adjust along the way.

Use a timer.

If you need to start a task and keep the momentum and focus going, set an alarm. In the back of my head, I seem to know that time is on the clock, which works to keep me focused and going.

Tick the completed tasks.

If you just can't start, tick all of the tasks you've done already.

> Woke up—*tick*
> Turned alarm off—*tick*
> Got up, got dressed—*tick*
> Made breakfast—*tick*
> Opened up the computer—*tick*

Whatever you have done, just write them down and tick them. Then ask yourself what you'd like to accomplish next—and do it. Often, it allows a flow to let you begin what you want to start.

Do something different for a distraction.

This technique has already been mentioned, but it's definitely worth the reminder. If you find yourself in your pattern and your normal reaction to this pattern is a certain behavior, then the idea is to start to break the pattern. One simple thing you can do to reduce the hold that it has on you is to do something different than what you would normally do. So, if you would typically sit and continue to mull over the last conversation you had, trying to understand what went wrong, then maybe get up and walk outside or around the block instead. Or if your behavior is to call your friend who you know will help with the drama, then don't. Instead, make yourself a cup of tea, go for a walk, read a book, close down the computer, or turn your phone off.

It doesn't matter what it is that you do differently; just do something different. It helps to rejig the pattern enough to start seeing things in a different way or at least take the energy out of your reaction, which sends you on a different course and helps you see things clearer.

This technique can be helpful when you're not deep in the emotion of the pattern, but it still has a hold on you. Other layers to add that are helpful are grounding yourself (see Chapter 1), breathing (see Chapter 3), and reducing your anxiety (see Chapter 4). Review the steps in the previous chapter. It's important to acknowledge if you feel anxious to do so. By acknowledging it, it's the first step in reducing its effect.

LONG-TERM SOLUTIONS

Reduce the reactions that occur when faced with a task or decision. When reducing the intensity of our reactions, two techniques come to mind, so they reduce and stay reduced. They will always be there, but it's easier to ground and refocus when they are not so intense.

One technique was discussed in Chapter 3—the *Ho'oponopono* prayer.

Tapping, or the Emotional Freedom Technique (EFT), is another technique that enables us to reduce the intensity of our body reactions and patterns to get grounded and live the life of our dreams.

Tapping (EFT)

Emotional Freedom Tapping (EFT) was developed by Gary Craig. You can find different varieties or ways to do this, but the commonality between them is similar. EFT is a tapping technique that works on meridian points. It helps to reduce the intensity of the patterns in your body. It is an effective way to reduce physical and emotional pain.

Acupoint stimulation (Emotional Freedom Techniques, EFT) has previously resulted in significant changes in stress biochemistry and psychological distress symptoms in a clinical trial, and this replication study confirmed the original outcomes: that one hour of tapping on acupoints results in a significant decrease in the stress hormone cortisol. From research, it's been shown to affect fear, anxiety, depression, stress, and physical pain. It helps alleviate psycho-emotional discomfort, reduce cortisol levels (affecting stress) and PTSD symptoms, improve the immune system, increase productivity, and many other things. According to Dr. Mark Hyman, a physician, and thirteen-time *New York Times* best-selling author, "Tapping is one of the most directed and powerful ways to peel away those layers of chronic stress."[9]

The technique involves tapping on specific independent points in a particular sequence while speaking a phrase. There are a few variations of the phrase you can say as you tap on the points; however, the one I use is below for reference.

Even though _____(Fill in the blank with an issue you want to focus on. It could be general or specific. Some examples of issues include general lack of money, general anxiety, reduce stress, etc.), *I still love and adore myself.*

Issues you might consider include, "I don't know how I'm going to pay my bills this month," or "If I Step Up, I'll be alone." Fill in the blank with an issue that is relevant in your life right now.

I have taken the following diagram on the tapping point sequence from Jayne Leonard's "What Is EFT Tapping? Evidence and How-to Guide," but it's available in many references.[10] Use the diagram to go along with the below steps.

- Choose a focus phrase and consider the issue you have chosen. How would you rate it on an intensity level from 0–10?

- Begin tapping the karate chop point on one hand with the other. Repeat three or four times.

- Use two or more fingertips to tap on each individual point on the body in sequence while repeating the phrase you selected. Tap each point around five times each.

- For this example, we'll use the following phrase. *Even though I don't know how I'm going to pay my bills this month, I still love and adore myself.*

Figure E

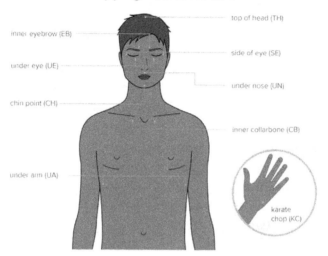

Follow the sequence of points below.

- Top of the head (TOH)—directly in the center of the top of the head

- Beginning of the eyebrow (EB)—the beginning of the brow, just above and to the side of the nose

- Side of the eye (SE)—on the bone at the outside corner of the eye

- Under the eye (UE)—on the bone under the eye, approximately one inch below the pupil

- Under the nose (UN)—the point between the nose and upper lip

- Chin point (CH)—halfway between the underside of the lower lip and the bottom of the chin

- Beginning of the collarbone (CB)—the point where the breastbone (sternum), collarbone, and first rib intersect

- Under the arm (UA)—at the side of the body, approximately four inches below the armpit

While some points—for example, the EB, SE, and UE—have a twin point on the other side of the body, it is only necessary to tap on one side. However, individuals can tap these points on both sides if both of their hands are free.

Again, you tap five times on the acupressure points as you say the phrase in the correct sequence.

I usually do a few rounds of this, then retest the intensity of my stress or anxiety on the 0–10 scale. You're looking for a reduction in the intensity number and want it to decrease to less than two or plateau.

Sometimes, the phrase may change the more you work on it. I have found the body can have more specific phrases that are held in the body. Don't be too concerned about the phrasing to start. If during the technique, it feels it could be better worded another way, then go with it. You can play with different wording to see if a phrase has more of an effect.

What I love about this technique is that it is highly effective as it works on your body's reaction to your beliefs.

HOMEWORK

Pick a recent or current task you're focused on.

Part A

- Have you had issues with finishing a task?

- If so, what have you been experiencing? What happens? What are your actions around the task? What are you feeling?

- What works for you to complete the task? Can you complete the task? What are the consequences of this choice?

- Do you need to make any decisions?

Perform the Technique

- Breathe and ground yourself if you can.

- Focus on the task and rate the intensity of how you feel about it on a scale of 0–10.

- Pick a focus phrase to practice the EFT technique.

- With the sequence of the tapping points in front of you, start tapping the sequence, tapping on each individual area five times with two or more fingertips.

- Say, "Even though (phrase), I still love and adore myself."

- Repeat for a few cycles of the sequence and review your number on the intensity scale.

- Continue until it reaches less than two or the number has plateaued.

Part B

- Review the task at hand. How do you feel about it? Has anything changed?

- This is a process and may take many times to work, depending on the level of difficulty you're having and the reason you are finding it challenging to complete the task.

- Make sure you review the other short term solutions to help you complete the task

- Use this process for any issue and physical or emotional pain.

To best assimilate the lessons you've just read and capture their full effect, please complete the homework before moving on to the next chapter.

6

ANGER AND BOUNDARIES

*He who has conquered anger has
achieved a great victory in life.*

—Gandhi

I f we are angry, are we aware that we are? Because we deny emotions so well, we aren't often mindful that we're angry. If we are, are we merely mad at ourselves, angry at others, or has some boundary been crossed?

Anger is a common emotion that's generally poorly dealt with in our society and can be very destructive and hurtful. When dealt with well, anger can be a very powerful motivator, providing amazing energy to help us move forward. When not dealt with well, it's destructive to the person and others around them and can often be expressed as rage or suppressed causing depression.

For the perfectionist, anger is a constant emotion. We can be angry by reacting to something external, our internal Inner Critic's ongoing analysis of our situation, or our boundaries having been crossed. Whatever the cause, in this emotional space, your body isn't grounded. You're more in your head and not in your authentic self.

The Inner Critic is negative and persistent, and if you listen to what it is telling you (i.e., what you are telling yourself), it's often attacking. This self-hatred leads to anger. Externally, we can find ourselves reacting with anger to others or situations. What I respond to is not often the same as what you react to. Sometimes, people irritate us beyond reprieve, yet they don't affect others the way they affect us. Our driver is the same, but our reaction may look different depending on our socialization, traumas, and experiences. For example, I react to stupidity with an instant reflex of my eyes rolling in the back of my head and a feeling of rage. Others may also react to this same trigger but with different intensities and ways.

Perfectionists will try to control and monitor anger according to being correct and perfect. This is often unconscious. We become very black and white, and our actions illustrate the need to follow the rules. To the observer, we could be walking with short, sharp steps like those on a mission. There is no time for pleasantries. In my experience, things need to be done promptly, and there's no time to waste on small talk or stupidity. Spoken words can be blunt and very nasty. We often don't realize when we are angry—our body is tense, but we aren't aware of this. We still feel fine; our smile is still on our faces. The smile, however, isn't a reflection of joy; it's simply a mask that's false based on the nature of it and the incongruence with our body and actions.

In this space, we can lack openness and are very disconnected from our hearts. The perfectionist doesn't realize the mask they are putting on is quite obvious to everyone.

When anger isn't acknowledged, it escalates in energy and comes out sideways or gets stuck in our bodies. Passive aggression is anger coming out sideways in the form of our blunt and short sentences and our sarcastic and sly remarks under our breath. They can be quite clever but never spoken out loud directly to whoever it's about. It is palpable, though.

Other people can often feel the passive aggression rising, waiting for it to come out in some form, like sarcasm or a nasty burst of rage. If it stays in the body, it can result in disease, pain, and anxieties; the intensity can build up over the years.

As we get older, if we don't become aware and change our thoughts or question our beliefs, we will end up spending our time reacting to others instead of connecting to our authentic selves, speaking our truth, and following that path. Our well-worn patterns and overreacting behaviors can be intense and lead to inappropriate rage or attempts to control anger that result in passive aggression and exhaustion on our part. That behavior can feel cutting to those around us.

Anger feels like it gives us a sense of energy, like when we are righteous and passionate about a cause. We can use anger to help fuel our righteousness, which allows us to be angry for the sake of perceived good. This justifies our anger and not being perfect. Being so used to anger, this feels normal. It's not exactly healthy, though, and once we deal with the source of the anger and its triggers, we can start to become more grounded and directed.

RESENTMENT

Perfectionists try to measure up to the pressure of the internal critic's demands for excellence. They will feel driven to be good while internally judging those who disobey the rules.

—*Helen Palmer*

Perfectionists seem to be in a continual state of resentment. This is felt for those who don't share our need to follow the rules of correctness and don't align with correctness over pleasure. We find ourselves resentful, defined by the difference between needing to follow this sense of correctness and the desire to satisfy our Inner Critics' demands over any internal, real desire. It's held for others, too, who don't toe the line and do the same.

If, for example, we observe others taking shortcuts and not working as hard as we think they should, aren't following the rules, are taking unnecessary breaks, and are having fun when we think they shouldn't, then we may become resentful.

BOUNDARIES

When we fail to set boundaries and hold people accountable, we feel used and mistreated.

—*Brené Brown*

Creating healthy boundaries is empowering. By recognizing the need to set and enforce limits, you protect your self-esteem, maintain self-respect, and enjoy healthy relationships. Unhealthy boundaries cause emotional pain that can lead to dependency, depression, anxiety, and even stress-induced physical illness.

When boundaries are crossed, you can get many sorts of reactions, including anger. It takes practice to be aware when your thoughts and body are reacting to your boundaries being crossed.

Types of boundaries include mental, physical, material, sexual, intellectual, time, and emotional. I work with boundaries daily. Physically, this can be in the form of personal space. People have their own space around them where they feel comfortable and safe. If you respect their space, then you can communicate more effectively with them. If you don't respect it and move into it, you will notice their subtle reactions. They may move backwards, slightly away from you with their body, or they may show signs of anxiety and confusion. It's helpful to see and observe their reactions and move to a place that falls within their comfort zone because the person may not be aware and may not be able to tell you.

If you don't respect their space, they are less able to hear you; they have a sense of anxiety that can make it difficult for them to concentrate and communicate effectively with you. If you wish to have a meaningful conversation with people, want them to hear what you're saying, and for them to think and discuss what you have to say, then it's better for you to remain outside their personal space.

If I observe a person move their body unconsciously away from me, then I move further back until I feel or see them relax. Then I know they can hear me.

Horses are fabulous at showing you how to feel boundaries and then respect them. If you move closer to an animal or human, then you need to respect their boundaries. If they move close or into yours, then they need to respect yours. If you want the best outcome for connection and communication, you need to understand physical boundaries.

For maximum connection and communication, do the following:

- Ask permission before you approach or touch them. After all, you're entering their space.

- Be aware of their body's reactions to your presence.

- Be aware of how they are saying things and thinking.

- Observe their body movements.

If you're in someone else's physical space and they move unconsciously away from you, if they have difficulty following what you are saying or seem uncomfortable or anxious, you're too close. You should move further away from them until you feel or see them relax and engage. That space varies from person to person, but when you are too close, there is a physiological reaction, and people lose the ability to hear, concentrate, and talk, and if your desire is to have an in-depth conversation and connect with them, then they are unable to do so when you are this close. It's thus important to read the signs.

Some people don't understand personal space, and others do but use it to their advantage. For example, sometimes you must deal with someone that may impose on your personal space and doesn't realize the effect this has on you. For these people, you simply need to ask or motion them to move back or move back yourself. Others may like to dominate your space and enjoy intimidation. These people often respect being stood up to, but to do this can be quite intimidating and difficult because they are in your space, which increases your physiological reaction. You literally find it harder to hear and converse, and it perhaps brings up anxiety, making it even more difficult to want to confront them. For these people, however, standing up to them is respected. If you don't, these people will keep pushing your boundaries, invading your personal space. To do this, we need to focus on breathing.

As long as it is safe to do so, when approached by someone like this, you need to stand your ground and breathe instead of removing yourself from their space. Breathing will help you calm down your internal reactions while not backing down in their eyes. Hold this space as long as you can, then move away. This can be terribly confrontational, so only do what you feel you can do and look after yourself.

This is a muscle and takes practice.

Try again next time. Confidence grows with practice. Remember only to do this, though, if it's safe. Try not to move backwards, stand your ground, and breathe.

HOMEWORK

Part A

When next talking with someone, make observations:

- Notice their body reactions, how they're acting, and how well they're listening and understanding you. Are they engaged in what you are saying? Or do they seem uncomfortable or nervous?

- Be aware of their body movements.

- Move towards them and continue to notice their mannerisms. Do they physically move or change behavior? Where is your personal space with this person?

- Learn to feel that zone between where they are and aren't comfortable being in your space.

Part B

Try this with a variety of people and not only notice their reactions but also pay attention to how you react—where you are comfortable and where you are not. This point will be different with different people. Use this information to connect and communicate better with others.

To best assimilate the lessons you've just read and capture their full effect, please complete the homework before moving on to the next chapter.

7

THE RIGHT WAY

Self-righteousness has killed more people than smoking.

—John McCarthy

While watching a musical theatre performance of *Dirty Dancing* with friends, the words, which were verbatim from the movie, seemed irritatingly wrong to me. With a fresh irritation watching it at the musical, I had to say something. I turned to my friend sitting next to me to say just how wrong the words were and how they should be. The way I said it was with such anger and bluntness, you'd think it would've been the next important thing to discuss at parliament. It had to be said. Everyone should know. I just couldn't let it go.

After stating my opinion, her reaction told me maybe not everyone agreed with me. In my mind, though, I was still right. I checked myself, as maybe her reaction was because I hadn't expressed it perfectly in my tirade. *Mind your tongue and don't say it again,* I said to myself. I'll never forget the look on her face, her weird, irritated frown. The look said, "Who really cares?" Without a word, she turned her back on me and walked away. I wanted to respond and say, "I know, I know, I know. But it still had to be said. You don't understand. It was wrong!"

Clearly, no one else could see it, so I needed to be the one to tell them.

I know what you're thinking. *Why waste so much energy getting so worked up over this?* Well, in my mind, it was wrong, and people needed to know. I couldn't let it go. In this example, there was a sense of importance that needed to be voiced. People needed to hear it. And if it falls on ears that don't recognize it, it often needs repeating until it's heard and validated.

As I've already mentioned, being right is one of the favorite traits of the perfectionist. It's not like we try to be correct and play on that trait; it's just that we are. Well, in our minds, we are. In truth, there are many ways to do things; we just can't see them. Others can have their right way, and it can be different to ours. The fact that we can't see this is the problem. We can't see another way, only ours. Our focus is on being correct—it's very black and white.

The right way can be so consuming that it fully occupies our minds. It's very important. We become transfixed on the thought and need to find a way for it to be received. In this space, there's no way we can hear what others say, or we simply dismiss what others say. We are correct. Our world revolves around being right and perfect. Perfection and control, then, require us to say it at the ideal time and in the perfect way, which may involve suppression and overthinking. There's so much to consider. Still, though, a lot of this reaction is unconscious. We're just aware of our opinion and that we are right.

The emotional charge that is attached to being right means we will defend this at all costs. Often, the battle is fought to defend our opinion and be right even though after discussion, we know we are not. I'm not saying that we're wrong; I'm saying the attachment to us being correct is the problem.

Being correct is needed. We don't like to fail and will argue our point. Sometimes it feels like it's a matter of life and death.

We are good at negating what others say. After all, we're great at pulling details into pieces. We can put so much energy into being right that we forget the importance of our bigger goals and dreams and that being right isn't helping.

Thus, the need to be right can come with a lot of anger, sarcasm, passive aggression, nastiness, and bluntness. We argue for the sake of arguing because of our attachment to needing to be right. We will do what it takes to save face. The lengths we can go to prove this can far outweigh the value of the point. It takes a bigger person to let go of needing to be correct and, right or wrong, take a step back and see the bigger picture, let go of what others think, and let go of the need to be right.

In conversation with my perfectionist friend, I was discussing the need for perfectionists to find the line of balance. To find that line of enough is enough, that the task is done well enough, and to let go of the tweaking. I was aware—with a smile on my face—that though we had the same understanding, the way he was describing it was right. He didn't think my way was wrong, but his was more right, and I needed to acknowledge it. Both our points needed to be accepted by the other, which required the other person to stop making their point and concede. Then they would be happy. It wasn't enough to acknowledge each opinion.

Without experience and maturity, there was no way either of us was conceding. After some time, we would drop the discussion. From experience and life, you learn that continuing to argue your point gets you nowhere except angry. But secretly, each of us wanted to be right. Making that point and being correct felt like the most important thing. We can still try our utmost to be more right. Eventually, I smiled and let go of needing to persist with the discussion. Here, there's an attachment to making the point, needing to be correct, and for our point to be heard.

Without the attachment of needing to be correct, other ideas can surface and be considered. I no longer waste energy fighting for something that takes me away from what matters, from the bigger picture and open discussions. Little arguments about irrelevant things in life aren't necessary and save me valuable energy and focus. What I need to do instead is to surrender, let go, and ground myself.

HEALING PROCESS

According to Roger Gabriel, chief medical officer for Deepak Chopra:

> Spiritual surrender is referred to as the "joy of surrender." It is the wonderful, positive feeling you have when you simply let go. It's stepping out of all limitations, expanding beyond your usual conditioning, and opening to infinite possibilities. It's offering up the small self or personal identity to that of the absolute.[11]

Surrendering isn't a bad thing. In fact, when you surrender, you let go of how it is. How is it when you're in the thick of it? Is it like you're in this belief and this pattern? Letting go of that paradigm means you can live outside of it. It doesn't mean you are relinquishing power or submitting. It is, in fact, quite the opposite. It's a space where you are outside of all of your thoughts and feelings and ways things need to be. The space enables you to let go and ground, be in a place where you can see more objectively, listen to life from a grounded space, make more enlightened decisions, and be able to hear and follow your intuition and higher purpose. Sometimes, it feels whenever you are in the thick of your pattern reactions, letting go gives away all your passion and power. It does not, believe me.

To Surrender

When trying to surrender for the first time, you can make it a more powerful experience by using your imagination. As you get better at this, the process and ability to release becomes easier.

So, take a big breath. Imagine you're tying all your thoughts, reactions, anger, decisions, and whatever you are thinking and feeling at that moment into a cloth in front of you. Here, it would be all your anger and right-way thoughts and feelings. Now, imagine wrapping it all up and tying it with a secure knot. Hold it in front of you and, with a big swoop of your arms, imagine releasing it high into the sky. Smile and say goodbye. They are gone, and you are free. Breathe and then come back to your body and breathe again.

Sometimes, when you are in the thick of the emotion of your patterns, surrendering can be difficult. After all, this takes effort to let go of the thoughts and feelings driving you—letting go and surrendering all that need to be right and proving to the world that you are correct is difficult. But they are driving you and maintaining you in the same pattern you do over and over again. So, practice surrendering all day. When you cannot make a decision, find that you're procrastinating, or need to be right, just let it go. You'll find the more you can let go and surrender, the easier it is to do because you'll feel the grounded power of your higher purpose more and more and will appreciate how fulfilling that feels over any of your limiting views and patterns.

HOMEWORK

Name a scenario when you felt you were right and were hanging on, unwilling to let go of what you were thinking.

Part A

- What were you being right about?

- On a scale of 0–10 (Zero being not important and ten being the most important), how important was it to get this viewpoint across?

- What were you thinking and feeling at the time?

- What action did these thoughts and feelings drive you to do?

- If nobody heard you or understood you and took on what you said, would that matter?

- If yes, why?

- Imagine wrapping all those thoughts, feelings, and actions up in a cloth in front of you.

- Tie a knot around it so all is secure.

- Imagine sending this high into the air with a big swoop, letting it all go, surrendering it high into the sky.

- Ground yourself and breathe.

Part B

Ask the following questions (close your eyes if you feel safe to do so):

- Was this "right" opinion important to be said in the grand scheme of things?

- What are you thinking and feeling now?

- What's important now?

- What are you learning about yourself? About the action of surrendering?

- What can you do next towards following your higher purpose?

- Next time this happens, when and how can you change your reaction?

- In the future, what can you use as an awareness tool when you may be in your "right way" pattern? It could be a feeling, a body reaction, a thought, or an awareness of how others are behaving. When you notice this, you can surrender quicker and stay grounded and on track more easily.

Remember, we're letting go and surrendering to the attachment of being correct. What you are offering may be a valid opinion. It's when that opinion needs to be heard at all costs that makes it limiting and non-productive. Making it more correct and needing to be seen that way by others can often be a waste of energy —time to surrender the attachment, ground yourself, and review the situation. From a grounded space, it's easier to review your next step, whether that be letting go and dropping it altogether or finding different, more grounded ways to refresh your thoughts.

To best assimilate the lessons you've just read and capture their full effect, please complete the homework before moving on to the next chapter.

8

CONTROL

I'm not a control freak—I'm a control enthusiast.

—Joss Whedon

At all costs, appearances need to be maintained. We need to maintain that mask.

Being a non-predatory animal, a horse has monitored you and your reactions long before you become aware of them standing there. You enter their field; they know exactly how you are feeling. They must as being a non-predatory animal like a deer, they need to work out if you are going to eat them, if you're dangerous, or if you are okay and they can trust you. They can sense your incongruence, which means your mask isn't saying what you are actually feeling. As in any situation as a perfectionist, the mask or façade of perfection needs to be portrayed at all costs. To achieve this, thoughts, feelings, actions, and emotions need to be suppressed. Horses sense suppressed emotions and thoughts, and until you acknowledge the feelings, they will continue to perceive the heightened energy around you and can be wary of you.

Say, for example, you have an argument in the morning with your partner before going to see your horse. (If you don't own a horse, bear with me through this example.) You don't deal with the emotion. You push it down and suppress it and put a smile on your face like everything is fine. But everything isn't okay. The look on your face isn't a joyous smile, but more of a tight-lipped line, and you're walking like there's a fire in you, still churning over the morning's argument. The observant person can see the incongruence between the smile, what they feel coming from you, and your actions. The anger is very palpable despite the smile on your face. To the horse, all they sense is the suppressed emotion and anger and that it's buried and not acknowledged—it's still palpable.

My horse reacts to that with equal intensity. She doesn't trust me and is wary of me. Instead of coming to me with heart from a grounded space, she may move in the opposite direction away from me with her ears pricked back, waiting for the *potential* onslaught from my anger. She won't come over to me until I am congruent and grounded, meaning she will not connect with me until I acknowledge the suppressed emotion and am more in my heart. Only in that space can she feel the intensity of the emotion go. It is still there, but she no longer needs to be concerned about how I will react—she feels safe to connect with me. Other horses will respond differently, but they will be on guard until you have dropped the emotion and façade and become congruent, authentic, and grounded.

People are the same. If the person can sense your anger but notes your smile, they will react differently to you than if you have acknowledged the emotion and are more grounded. Most people on some level sense this difference but may not register it consciously as the way we engage depends on how you have been taught by society's norms. On this unconscious level, you present as confusing. Your mask and how you present don't match; you aren't authentic and are incongruent. In society, we aren't taught how to be congruent. How people react to you depends on their conditioning. They could be quite wary like the horse. What you portray to others can be felt. Unlike the horse, though, we will often try to connect with you regardless of your authenticity and follow social norms. Of course, it's always your choice to connect with someone or not, but if they are a work colleague or boss, then you have to find a way. A horse will choose not to engage.

How wonderful would it be if we all could be congruent and authentic and just connect with others from this grounded space? Connection, communication, and relationships would be more authentic and powerful. The issue for perfectionists especially is we don't realize when we're incongruent. Suppressing emotion is like breathing for us. It is so routine that we need to be shown when this isn't the case. Animals like horses are great for this. Children, too, before they are socialized, can be great mirrors. I'm not saying buy a horse or lease a child, but we need to be more aware.

Another example is fear. If someone is feeling fearful, they're more likely to hold their breath. A fearful person will breathe shallowly and can hold their bodies quite tightly and in stress. On a physiological level, their blood pressure, heart rate, and other stress reactions have increased. Horses can sense all of this, which heightens their response to you. The horse may think, *What is dangerous? What can you see that I can't? Why the fear?* People react too; it may not, however, be as obvious.

As soon as you acknowledge your fear for yourself, you take with it the heightened reaction and the tenseness of your body. You may acknowledge this fear to yourself or out loud, but as soon as you do, you'll notice that you're breathing differently, your blood pressure and heart rate have also decreased, and you have relaxed somewhat. If you're with a horse, it will react differently to you too. They are relaxed and are breathing more normally. You're now more congruent. It doesn't mean you're no longer fearful; it's just the intensity in the energy has lessened. You're more congruent with your presence and have dropped the mask, acknowledging the fear instead of suppressing and projecting it.

In our stressful lifestyles, we often have no idea how stressed and anxious we are. Stress is a significant cause of death, and we generally don't realize an elevated level of stress has become our new normal. We live with this suppressed stress reaction in our bodies, which we chronically project out to others. This stressed state changes how people and animals relate to us. By becoming congruent through acknowledging our suppressed feelings, we can change the reactions of others. By doing so, we not only affect our own health and connection to our grounded state, but we encourage more authentic connections, communications, and relationships with others.

As humans, we're conditioned by society and often aren't aware of our incongruencies, though we can sense them. Most of that is unconscious, and we behave how society has shown us. Horses and animals simply connect with their heart from a grounded space. They don't have agendas, nor are they socially conditioned. If they have a choice and don't have to deal with you, then they won't. Humans will. Humans have to attempt to communicate with you and be in a relationship with you to work with you. You'll find it easier to be with others, however, and have deeper, more heartfelt connections if you're more grounded and not suppressing your emotions.

We need to work out how to be congruent and authentic inside and out. When we are harmonious and genuine, we can connect to our true selves rather than reacting like a perfectionist trying to control everything and maintain perfection. We can release or surrender rather than suppress and control, affecting our paths, relationships, and connections with others. We are more able to connect to ourselves and our higher purpose and follow our dreams. It's not healthy to hold on to things—we didn't need to push it down in the first place. What we need to do is acknowledge our emotions and not try to control them.

Linda Kohanov, in her book *The Power of the Herd,* explains in elaborate detail the effects of emotions and suppressed and contagious emotions:

> "When emotions are suppressed over the long term, they intensify into other, more troublesome complexes and impulses, eventually causing people to act out in unproductive ways when the pressure reaches critical mass, sometimes damaging relationships irreparably."[12]

EMOTIONS ARE CONTAGIOUS

I went to a festival a few years ago. It was a wonderful experience, and like any other large event of this caliber, there were lots of tired, drunk people at the end finishing their last dances and chats and trying to get to their car or mode of transport home. The last performance was clever. On stage, Tibetan monks sang. I don't know if you have experienced any music of this kind, but it is on a lower, calmer, grounded wavelength. People stopped, sat, and calmed down. When the monks finished, the energy of the crowd changed. No longer was it hyped and out for more fun—it became calm and patient. And with that, everybody moved in an orderly fashion to their mode of transport with no arguments or incidents.

If you are grounded, you can help others to find this space. Have you ever noticed if you are in the presence of someone who is grounded, after a while, you start to feel less anxious and flighty and become more grounded? The opposite is also true. Sometimes, it takes a lot of energy to stay grounded and follow your intuition when those around you are anxious or emotional. This is more difficult when you're finding it challenging to stay grounded yourself.

HEALING PRACTICE

This practice is a way to be aware of emotions that you are potentially suppressing and how others may be reacting to you.

- Take notice of the emotions surrounding you—either from others or yourself.

- If you feel an emotion, then simply announce to yourself or someone you trust that you're feeling this emotion. It can be anything from anger, fear, shame, guilt, joy, love, annoyance, embarrassment, depression, sadness, rage, stuck, or frozen, to name a few. If you don't feel anything, that's also okay—just notice. There may be an emotion under it. Just allow it and don't overanalyze it.

   Whether or not the emotion is internal (you are reacting to your own patterns and beliefs), allow it to be there without being attached to what it means. Be prepared for the intensity to increase as you are now allowing it to be there, and you are not suppressing it—just because you can feel it more because you're not suppressing it doesn't mean everybody else can. Remember, a feeling cannot hurt you.

- If the emotion is external (being from another person), try to locate the source. For a further explanation of internal and external sources, see Chapter 9 under "Reactions."

- Don't stress too much on finding the source, just feel the emotion, practice letting go and surrendering.

- Connect to an authentic, grounded space.

- Breathe.

Play with connecting to yourself by grounding yourself and seeing the effect it has on those around you. You might be surprised at how it can change.

*If you've suffered trauma in the past or if the homework exercises are overwhelming, then it may be helpful to practice them with a supportive professional.

HOMEWORK

This section of Homework will help you look at how people are responding and connecting to you before and after acknowledging, letting go, and surrendering the emotion.

Part A

- Acknowledge what you are thinking and feeling. What action is this driving you to do?

- Simply acknowledge the thoughts and feelings to take the power out of them and breathe.

- Surrender, breathe, and ground yourself.

- Connect to others from this grounded, authentic space.

Part B

- Notice your feelings now? Have they changed? For example, have they changed in intensity, or are they the same? Just notice. Are there any differences in how you see the world and those in it?

- Are people reacting differently? Are you reacting differently?

- What do you notice about yourself, thoughts, feelings, and actions?

- What will you do differently from this mindset?

The exercises in "I See Me" from Chapter Two may also be of benefit to review to see how you are reacting and how others are reacting to you.

Our aim is to be in our higher purpose, listen to our intuition, and follow where it takes us. It's easier to do this if our beliefs aren't as loud, which is why I've spent so much time showing the importance of decreasing their effect. Don't lose sight of the bigger picture and your dreams. We are to refocus whenever we can, hear our intuition, and take action on it so we can nudge ourselves forwards towards our higher purpose. It's definitely a journey but one worth following. Though it's important to accept who we are, it's also important to follow who we are meant to be.

Another way to help find our higher purpose is to meditate and ask to receive what that might be.

For extra support, I have created a guided visualization for you to follow. Simply tap on the link and download.

https://linktr.ee/kristenableson

To best assimilate the lessons you've just read and capture their full effect, please complete the homework before moving on to the next chapter.

9

CHRONIC SUPPRESSION

*Unexpressed emotions will never die. They are buried
alive and will come forth later in uglier ways.*

—Sigmund Freud

The long-term effects of suppressing emotions take
their toll. It is not a healthy practice by any means
and can lead to more intense reactions to our patterns
and behaviors.

CONSEQUENCES OF CONTROL
AND SUPPRESSION

- Exhaustion—it takes a lot of energy to keep
  everything in check.

- Passive aggression, sarcasm, curt remarks, and rage
  are anger coming out sideways. Frustration is chronic
  anger not dealt with. Fear and anxiety show in body
  reactions.

- Some people shake, and some are quiet, but you can often feel it. The constant denial of anger can lead to sadness and depression.

- Avoiding speaking to avoid saying the wrong thing—to be not perfect but also to avoid hurting others. From an authentic and grounded space, it's easier to speak your truth and speak from your heart.

- Overthinking and mental anguish

- Increase in anger and resentment

- Increase of reactions in body and body patterns

- Always needing to have that perfection mask on—which means it is difficult to relax and just be who you really are.

- Limited and poor relationships and connections with people

- Chronic illness

The chronic denial of emotions results in the suppressed emotions we allow to gain energy and intensity and take up space in our bodies. They gain more power and intensity by us not acknowledging them and by attempting to control and ignore them.

Take, for example, my issues with the musical. Those irritations and annoyances weren't ever dealt with and were cleverly pushed down and out of my mind, taking up space in my body. Viewing the musical triggered it all—the injustice, the wrongness, the need for it to be said. And before I knew it, it all came out.

Suppressed emotions can come out sideways, and with emotional attachment, they tend to come out with more energy and intensity. It was also necessary for me to tell my "right way" belief in that example. The combination of belief and suppressed emotion in my pattern led to me reacting with intensity.

That musical scenario wasn't too bad or hurtful. The comment from the memory came out with some intensity, and because she didn't agree with it, she ignored me. I still felt ashamed, though.

In other scenarios, the intensity of my reaction can be quite different. The comment from the past event has greater emotional attachment. They can be unbelievably hurtful and damaging. Rage, anxiety, tears, screams, and destruction can pour out. Comments that are quite irrelevant in your life now have been festering and can come out with added intensity. They generally don't come out perfectly nor at an appropriate time.

People can feel attacked and uncomfortable because of our outbursts, and we can feel awful and ashamed. The suppression of the attached emotions and our patterns add to the intensity of our reactions towards people and our scenarios.

We react to people and situations all of the time. I was reacting to the musical. I respond with greater intensity due to the suppressed emotions and pattern of needing to tell others about the right way. This perfectionist belief causes me to act a certain way—this is my behavior, and I've been doing it for years. Now, I have the added energy of past, undealt with, suppressed emotions with their intensity on top of that. All of these cause me to react to people and scenarios in the present time. I react with intensity from all of these inputs.

Figure F

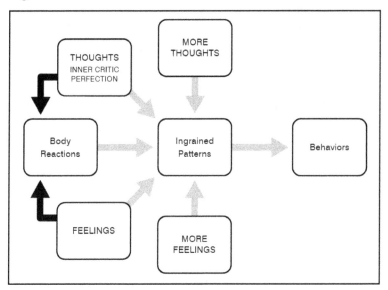

Note that Figure F is Figure B from Chapter 1 with the added thoughts and feelings sections. It shows that our ingrained patterns that have been set up for years get further ingrained by the addition of the same thoughts and feelings. This continues until we change the input and break up our ingrained patterns.

If I am to decrease the intensity of these reactions, I need to break up these patterns and their power. I need to reveal these suppressed, charged emotions in a healthy way and the way I think about it all. My desire is to react less to people, so they have less effect on taking me away from my higher purpose.

PATTERNS

After being a physiotherapist for near thirty years, I have seen firsthand the effect of emotional suppression and patterns as life's stresses and belief systems trigger them. They can present as chronic pain, injury, stress, and tension.

People with chronic pain often present with pain worsening from the same scenarios or stresses. Most of the time, they're unaware of their reoccurring pattern but can see how it starts and how it affects their behavior when it's pointed out to them. Certain relationship stresses in their life or money stress can affect them. They can present with headaches, joint or muscular pain, or simply posture issues caused by tiredness or overwork. Neck pain and headaches have been self-attributed to their late nights. Other contributors can be more subtle but consistent. Late nights coincide with money issues, relationship changes, family dramas, and eating habits. It could just be old family dramas. Maybe their sister's illness has set off old patterns that bring up unresolved emotions and behaviors. It can present as anything, including anxiety, headaches, and chronic pain depending on the patterns and past for that person.

Chronic pain affects our nervous system. Pain increases the sensitivity of the nervous system, activating the flight or fight reactions from the sympathetic nervous system branch. This can increase anxiety, blood pressure, and heart rate issues, with added pain, stress, and fear. Our patterns, traumas, and fears can also increase our chronic pain behaviors brought on by the effects of this heightened nervous system. Until we start to be aware of these causes, we will fall in peril to the chronic pain cycle and how it affects our lives.

Instead, we need to be aware of our individual patterns— which decreases the sensitivity of the nervous system—start to face our fears, and break down those patterns and causes of our reactions. Activating our parasympathetic nervous system via controlled breathing is a great way to counter the effects of the flight reaction. We also need to address, amongst other things, those patterns and thought processes that limit our behaviors and cause our bodies to react and respond as they do.

For my own body, I notice a familiar pattern of pain when I'm stressed. My hips would tighten, making it painful and difficult to run and keep fit. My jaw and thoracic spine ultimately gave me a headache, and my right shoulder ached. When trying to get fit, which I akin to Stepping Up and fully being in the world, my body always stopped me with fear, pain, and dysfunction. Realizing this, I addressed my anxieties, fears, and patterns. There are many layers to this, but awareness was a great start. The patterns have been there for many years, so the body patterns were thick and needed to be broken up and new ones formed. The result is a body that no longer tightens at my hip, my pelvis remains symmetrical, and I have the strength to allow me to run.

REACTIONS

You can react internally to your Internal Critic, feelings, and body reactions or externally towards others and situations.

For example, if we say something in a meeting, our Inner Critic will judge it. We could linger on what the reaction was, what others said, or how well we did based on how others behaved. Was this perfect? How did we fail? Emotions and feelings are present and intense, causing us to behave as we have always done. Energy here is being wasted on things that aren't necessarily helpful in moving forwards. Our minds are full of our judgments and our body reactions elevated making it challenging for us to be open, grounded, and aware. It's difficult to connect to others and the higher purpose if our minds focus on something entirely irrelevant and our bodies react to our patterns.

Externally, there are people who rub us the wrong way. They irritate us yet they don't seem to affect others the way they affect us. They're not doing deliberate things (though they may be) to antagonize us, but there's just something about them causing us to react. If you are reacting in this situation, then simply there is something inside of you that needs reviewing. These people are merely a mirror for you, a gift if you like to shine light on whatever suppressed pattern or emotion you have buried. They bring light to something in you that needs acknowledging, something that has too much power and reactivity.

We don't necessarily need to know what it is and where it has stemmed from. We just need to diminish it—to break it up—so it has less effect on us so we can stay focused on our dreams. The more we can see people as opportunities or gifts to help us work on our reactions rather than viewing them as irritating individuals who we continue to blame for our reactions, the quicker we'll grow.

No matter what the source of our reaction, this is where the work needs to be done. To reduce them. When we do this the benefits are astounding.

We become empowered, more accountable for ourselves, and we stop blaming others for their responses and our behaviors. We stop being small and limited. We no longer misuse time worrying, suppress emotions, or waste energy keeping our perfect mask unscathed. It becomes easier to ground ourselves and connect to what matters.

For this, we need to remember that:

- We're responsible for our reactions, and others are responsible for theirs. We can't change their response. We can only change how we choose to be.

- When viewed this way, we stop blaming everyone else for our behaviors or how we feel. We become accountable and empowered.

How do we stop our reactions?

1) The first thing to do is notice when you find yourself responding. This may be a thought, feeling, irritation, emotion, or behavior. It could be positive or negative.

2) Before you react, don't. Just breathe.

You're triggered; you feel something, and it's uncomfortable, which causes you to take an action—this is your reaction. Human beings, in general, don't like to feel uncomfortable. Feelings tend to drive us to take action to get us away from that uncomfortable feeling.

Stopping this is easier said than done; however, your task is to sit in the feeling, the emotion only. Taking the action will lead you further into your well-worn pattern.

If you feel the need to comment to someone over coffee about something that irritated you, don't. If you're upset by something, and your reaction or action is to call someone or eat chocolate, don't. Don't do what you would typically do. Sit in that uncomfortable feeling and breathe. Be aware of what the action is that is driving you to want to take but don't do it.

The action may not be a physical one. It might be to place a smile on your face when you feel hurt or angry or start thinking you are stupid and hopeless when you feel shame or guilt. You are just trying to avoid the uncomfortable. When you sit in it and breathe, its intensity may initially increase, but it will eventually decrease. The next time in a similar situation, you will react less until you barely respond at all.

As a reminder, stay safe. If your action is to move away from danger, then please do so. Don't place yourself in unsafe circumstances. Safety is your primary concern.

Sometimes, the emotions can feel very intense and scary, especially when you're not used to experiencing them. It's important to note that feelings are unable to hurt you. They're just feelings. They may feel absolutely awful and incredibly intense, but they won't hurt you. If you are concerned and scared, it's advisable to seek professional help for support.

You're in control of this process and can remove yourself from the emotion whenever you want. Initially, you may wish to set a timer for ten minutes or what you feel comfortable with. After the timer goes off, you can evaluate how the process went. If you're unhappy or still concerned, head to a professional. If you were okay, when ready, try it again.

The emotion can increase in intensity. Sometimes, it can be so intense it can hurt or render you frozen. Keep breathing and staying in it—don't let it take you where you can't feel it anymore. Gradually, over time, the intensity will subside. This can take anywhere from seconds to hours. It will diminish in strength, and the urge to do the action will reduce. You can stop any time you want.

This is a powerful process—the aim is to wait until the intensity of the emotion has reduced and you have reduced the desire to take that action. You need to do it in your own time, in your own safe environment. If you don't feel comfortable trying, get some help.

When I first learned about and started to practice this concept, I noticed I responded to everything. I was constantly in a state of anger and annoyance, as no one did anything the right way, and I was so far from perfect it wasn't funny. Initially, I would start to be aware of when I retorted and would try to see what I was responding to. Then I would spend time in this space to reduce its intensity. I could only do a few minutes at a time for two reasons. One was due to the number of reactions I had, and I wasn't able to think clearly in this state. The second was because sitting in the energy of them was intense. Over time, I realized I responded less and less to people. I could catch the reaction earlier and earlier and not respond at all. I even started to laugh at how much I reacted and how much energy and time I had spent away from my true journey.

In Summary

Part 1

1) Am I in my pattern? Am I reacting to something or someone? Just notice.

   (Awareness is the key; with awareness, you can start to reduce the power of the patterns, change the way you think, and refocus your attention on your dreams.)

2) Don't take the desired action you want to take; don't react. Don't follow the pattern. Instead, stay in the emotion and just breathe. Be aware of what it wants you to do, of what you would normally do, and breathe—don't act on it. Set a timer, if necessary, and bring yourself out of the feeling whenever you wish—you're in total control of this process. Seek a professional to hold a space for you or guide you through this process if you feel it could be too overwhelming. You don't need to go into the trauma or into the belief; you just need to sit in the feeling.

Emotions are emotions. They can be strong, painful, and uncomfortable. We don't like uncomfortable, and we generally will do anything to avoid these feelings. Don't let the uncomfortable sensation drive you to move away from the emotion.

Emotions cannot hurt you. They represent pains from the past that show up when they're triggered. While they can certainly feel awful and intense, they can't harm you.

Stay in the emotion. By staying, you'll find the emotion may increase in intensity. It will eventually reduce in intensity. The next time you react, your response will be less intense. So, do it again. Gradually, you can stop reacting altogether. This process can take one time or a few—it depends on how heavily ingrained it is in you.

If you wish, seek some professional help, someone who will hold a space for you and guide you along the process.

The process is to sit in the emotion, stop the reaction, and breathe.

Part 2

For added effect, try sitting in the emotion and repeating the Hawaiian prayer discussed in Chapter 4:

I'm sorry
Please forgive me
Thank you
I love you

HOMEWORK

Pay attention to a recent time where you reacted to something or someone. What was its intensity out of ten? (Zero being no intensity and ten being the most intense.)

Part A

- What was your reaction? What were your thoughts, feelings, and body reactions?

- What was the action you wanted to do because of these feelings?

- Set a timer for ten minutes.

- Draw attention to the emotion, sit in it, and breathe.

- Be aware of what action you did or what that emotion wants you to do, allow yourself to acknowledge this, but continue to sit in the emotion.

- See if you can stay in this emotion for the duration of the ten minutes. If you can't, that's okay. Take a breath and stop the exercise.

- When the timer finishes, assess how you are. If you feel comfortable and safe to continue, then do so. If you don't, that's okay. Take a breath and stop the exercise.

If you know you've had any trauma or believe you may have in the past or if this exercise is overwhelming, then it may be helpful to practice this exercise with a supportive professional.

Part B

- What did you notice about the emotion when you continued to sit in it?

- What was the action the emotion wanted you to do? Is that what you usually do to avoid the emotion?

- Rerate the emotion on an intensity scale of 0–10.

(When you feel comfortable and in charge of the exercise, you can try without the timer.)

A more effective way to reduce the intensity of the reaction is to sit in the emotion and repeat the Hawaiian phrase introduced in Chapter 4.

- Note the intensity of the emotion at the beginning on a scale of 0–10. (Zero being no intensity and ten being the most intense.)

- After sitting in the emotion, add the Hawaiian prayer.

  I'm sorry

  Please forgive me

  Thank you

  I love you

- Review the intensity number. The desire is that it's less. Continue until you get the number around or below two or three out of ten.

To best assimilate the lessons you've just read and capture their full effect, please complete the homework before moving on to the next chapter.

FINAL THOUGHTS

Increase the Volume of Our Intuition and Decrease the Volume of Our Perfectionism

Our ultimate goals are to follow who we really are and be as authentic and congruent as possible in the process. To live a life following our dreams and be in our higher purpose. We aim to realize we aren't our perfectionism, our patterns, or beliefs systems, and we don't need to listen to our Inner Critic. We aim not to react to our internal reactions or those of others.

We have a higher purpose and a set of dreams that are often bigger than us. To claim this life that we will love, it's beneficial to drop the perfectionism façade and follow our intuitive signs.

As our patterns are a part of our identity, we cannot fully remove them. They are a part of us, and they will still be a lens that we see the world through, but they don't have to be what we focus on. We can make them less powerful, less reactive, and quieter. Then it's easier to ground ourselves, connect to our higher selves, and follow our intuition.

THE NEXT PHASE

We all want to have what we would love in this life. Our behaviors, thoughts, and feelings keep us small and separate from our higher selves and from connecting to our dreams via our intuition. This reduces our ability to connect with others and ourselves in a profound way—from being the person we're meant to be, striving for the goals we dream about.

From a perfectionist viewpoint, the qualities of righteousness and our desires to be perfect are common. The ways laid out in this book help us reduce the effects of our minds, patterns, and behaviors that keep us small and away from our higher purpose.

I think there's something in this book for everyone, but my focus has been on perfectionism as I am a perfectionist. Many of my clients, though, are not, but we all have in common a set of reactions, behaviors, and perceptions that are unique to us. These techniques I have described and the message, in general, are messages I believe all can hear. Perfectionists might present behaviorally differently, but the driver is always the same. It's important to be aware of all of our patterns and reactions so we can hope to change—if this is what we want to do. If you're happy with how you behave and connect, thank you for reading this book. I believe there's a soul inside all of us that wishes to guide us to the life we dream about, and it has nothing to do with keeping us perfect and making sure we control our emotions and do the right thing. A fully lived life can be scary and one that the Inner Critic will have some comment about, but it is worth the effort.

It's essential to be aware of what we tell ourselves and what we feel. Our thoughts and feelings set up body reactions and patterns. These cause us to react. We spend so much energy and time trying to deal with them and follow where they take us that we get side-tracked off the path of what's important. We need to decrease the volume of that Inner Critic and break up the patterns and body reactions, so we don't react as much. If we don't respond as much, it's easier to refocus away from where the patterns takes us and focus on the path our higher purpose wishes to guide us along.

The higher purpose via our intuition is quieter in volume than the Inner Critic and less addictive than the need to follow our patterns. It's hard to stay on the path when these two voices are loud and pulling us in different directions. The path, if you listen, is always there with a constant desire to guide us to our dreams. All we need to do is listen. Hence, the added need to do the following:

1) Break up our body reactions so they are less addictive and forceful.

2) Reduce the intensity and power of our feelings.

3) Change the way we think.

Benefits of living the life from your higher purpose include the following:

- More flow

- More pleasure and fun

- Connection to your empowered space, your higher purpose, and intuition

- Connection to your heart, your grounded space, and those of others

- Improved communication and relationships with others

- More empowered in your whole, grounded self

- Self-love

- Acceptance of self

- Attracting similar people into our lives—those of heart, truth, and love

- A life of more joy and less drama

- Easier to find compassion and love for self
- Easier to reduce attachment to judgment
- Permission to not be perfect
- Acceptance of others

CHOOSE GRATITUDE

The miracle of gratitude is that it shifts your perception to such an extent that it changes the world you see.

—*Dr. Robert Holden*

Gratitude is simply taking time to think about all the positive things rather than ruminating on the negatives. It's the expression of appreciation for what one has, warmth and goodness, and is a recognition of value independent of money. Research has linked gratitude with a wide range of benefits, including strengthening your immune system, improving sleep patterns, experiencing more joy and pleasure, increasing happiness and boosting your mental health.

As a practice, gratitude is another way that moves you out of your thinking and feeling and into a space where you can start to see things clearer. It's a helpful tool to maintain a grounded space, moving you outside of your thoughts, feelings, and patterns. When you are grateful, it's easier to shift your thoughts towards your dreams and not sit in the energy and severity of the feelings of your pattern. It's easier to refocus and stay focused because the pattern has a lesser pull on you.

It's a great practice to think of things you're grateful for when you're heavily into your thoughts. Though this can feel impossible sometimes, with practice, it gets easier and can really pull you out of your head. Try to feel them deeply so you can feel them in every cell of your body. I like to think of twenty as a practice every night before I go to bed. When

I first started this practice, I was so heavily into my negative, worthless state that getting out of bed and getting dressed were all I could think of being grateful for. Twenty isn't so hard for me these days.

REFOCUS TOWARDS OUR DESIRES, GOALS, AND VISIONS

Remember, *refocus* means instead of focusing on our Inner Critic and perfectionist ways, we focus on our higher purpose, ground ourselves, listen to our intuition, and take action on what it says. This will lead us towards our dreams.

> *When we take our eyes off our goals, anxiety, worry, and doubt immediately begin to take over. Stay focused on what matters most at all times. Picture yourself achieving your goals and what that feels like instead of the obstacles that you will experience along the way.*
>
> *—Matt Mayberry*

Experiences and reactions can often deafen us from hearing our higher purpose. It's important to refocus on what we desire, our goals, and visions. We want to sit in our dreams. For the perfectionist, as we often spend our lives working on being correct, we have no idea what we want or what our dreams are. There's no marvelous way to find this, but there are many ways to find out what it is.

If you're having trouble finding a solution and find yourself sitting in the same rut over and over again, try sitting in the solution, not the problem—meditate on it, journal it, sit in a grounded space, and receive the next action step to take. There are many ways to do this, and below are just a few:

- Focus and refocus on your vision or goal and what it feels, looks, and tastes like.

- Use your imagination to place yourself in the vision and imagine it has already happened.

- Believe it to be true.

- Keep choosing it and following it.

- Keep taking action toward it

This book has not really focused on how to create our dream or higher purpose visions; instead, we have focused on their importance, our need to refocus on them, and ways to help this process. Just listen for that intuitive guide, and you can't falter.

Lastly, remember how incredible you are and that your life matters. You're not just a perfectionist but an amazing mixture of those traits and patterns and an incredible higher power full of wonderful dreams. You have a greater purpose. You need to love and embrace all of who you are and live your life to the fullest, living every experience in every moment.

- Be aware of the thinking and the language you tell yourself.

- Be aware of your patterns and behaviors.

- Catch your pattern, catch your thinking.

- Change your pattern, change your thinking.

- Break up the patterns in your body and reduce your reactions.

- Choose gratitude.

- Refocus always.

- Choose to connect to yourself and others from a grounded space.

- Find your higher purpose and follow it.
- Talk from a space of truth.

And finally . . . *just breathe.*

BIBLIOGRAPHY

1   Palmer, Helen. *The Enneagram.* New York, NY: HarperCollins, 1988.

2   Prendergast, John. *In Touch*: How to Tune into the Inner Guidance of Your Body and Trust Yourself. Louisville, CO: Sounds True, 2015.

3   Gershman, Noah. "I Am the Very Worst Person on Earth and Other Myths: Understanding and Reconciling With the Inner Critic." Masters Thesis Pacifica Graduate Institute. Published March 5, 2020. delos-inc.com/articles-b/THESIS%20N.%20 Gershman%203_5.pdf.

4   Moon, Tom. "Four Liberating Questions," *The Work of Byron Katie* (blog), October 16, 2017, thework.com/2017/10/ four-liberating-questions.

5   Ignoffo, Matthew. "Improve Reading by Overcoming the 'Inner Critic.'" *Journal of Reading* 31, no. 8 (1988): 704–8. jstor.org/ stable/40032952.

6   "Meditation: In Depth." *NCCIH*. Accessed September 21, 2021. nccih.nih.gov/health/meditation-in-depth.

7   Sharma, Robin. *The Monk Who Sold His Ferrari.* UK: HarperCollins, 2012.

8   Williamson, Jennifer. "Ho'oponopono Prayer for Forgiveness, Healing and Making Things Right," *Healing Brave* (blog), July 23, 2019. healingbrave.com/blogs/all/hooponopono-prayer-for-forgiveness .

[8] "Science and Research." *The Tapping Solution.* Accessed September 21, 2021.

[9] Leonard, Jayne. "A guide to EFT tapping." *Medical News Today.* September 26, 2019. medicalnewstoday.com/articles/326434.

[10] Gabriel, Peter. "5 Ways To Surrender Spiritually Through Meditation." *Chopra.* January 4, 2019. chopra.com/articles/5-ways-to-surrender-spiritually-through-meditation.

[11] Kohanov, Linda. *The Power of the Herd: A Nonpredatory Approach to Social Intelligence, Leadership, and Innovation.* California: New World Library, 2011.

YOUR NEXT STEPS WITH BETTER THAN PERFECT

 ASSIMILATE AND REFLECT
Download Workbook

 REFOCUS AND DREAM
Download your Guided Visualisation

 HELPING TO GROUND
Download your Guided Visualisation

**Access these *free* resources at
https://linktr.ee/kristenableson**

ABOUT THE AUTHOR

Kristen Ableson loves connecting people to their higher purpose and passions—to what really matters. As a physiotherapist, she deals with the psychology and physical ailments of pain, people's fears, and patterns on a daily basis. She is an Eponaquest Master Herder Instructor, facilitating equine programs which shine light on people's blocks as well as the inner qualities they can tap into strengthen and empower their own leadership abilities. The program builds personal skills as well as a community of connectedness and mastery.

Kristen has struggled with chronic pain, depression, associated anxiety, and overwhelm. She has spent years uncovering how our thoughts, body-held traumas, and anxieties limit life. Today, a transformed woman, Kristen invests in others as a coach and mentor. She especially enjoys working with people who deal with perfectionist traits and helping them see their own blocks and ways through life. She lives in Brisbane, Australia.

CPSIA information can be obtained
at www.ICGtesting.com
Printed in the USA
BVHW070454310522
638437BV00007B/357